Mediation and Reconciliation of Interests in Public Disputes

Jean Poitras   Pierre Renaud

Forewords by David E. Matz and Guy Baron

CARSWELL
Thomson Professional Publishing

Canadian Cataloguing in Publication Data

Poitras, Jean, 1968-; Renaud, Pierre, 1962-
    Mediation and Reconciliation of Interests in Public Disputes

Translation of: La médiation et la réconciliation des intérêts dans les conflits publics.

Includes bibliographical references and index.
ISBN 0-459-23354-8

    1. Mediation. 2. Conflict management. 3. Organizational sociology.
I. Poitras, Jean, 1968-; Renaud, Pierre, 1962-. II. Title.

HM136.P6413 1997   303.6'9   C97-900675-9

Translation: Dialangue inc.

Photographs on back cover:
Huguette Martel (left); Chantal Lefebvre (right).

Product Development Manager: **Mathieu Boutin**
Manager, Editorial Group: **Brigitte Giguère**
Legal Writer: **Lambert Perron**
Content Editor: **Josée Lafontaine**

CARSWELL
Thomson Professional Publishing

One Corporate Plaza
2075 Kennedy Road
Scarborough, Ontario
M1T 3V4

Customer Service:
Toronto: 1-416-609-8000
Elsewhere in Canada/United States: 1-800-387-5164
Fax: 1-416-298-5082

*The new leader
is a facilitator,
not an order giver.*

John Naisbitt
*Megatrends: Ten New Directions
Transforming Our Lives*

ACKNOWLEDGEMENTS

We are indebted to Luce Asselin, Jacqueline LaBrie and Jean-François Longpré for their helpful comments on the manuscript.

Special thanks to Lise Paré-Renaud and Sylvie Roy, whose patience and attention to detail allowed us to see this project through.

TABLE OF CONTENTS

CHAPTER 1

A NEW MEANS OF MANAGING PUBLIC DISPUTES

CHAPTER 2

MEDIATION: CONCEPT AND MODEL

CHAPTER 3

THE MEDIATOR'S BASIC TASKS

CHAPTER 4

THE MEDIATION PROCESS

CHAPTER 6

ETHICS AND TRANSPARENCY

LIST OF FIGURES

CHAPTER 6

LIST OF TABLES

FOREWORD

This book is based on hope. It has to be. It's topic, the mediation of public policy disputes, rests almost solely on the optimism that a better way to resolve such disputes can be found, that in some measure it has already been found.

It has, of course, been long understood that public policy disputes, and more recently environmental disputes, are enormously expensive to work through. Worse, they produce results that satisfy almost no one - other, perhaps, than those who want no change, no resolution. Mediation is thus implicitly a critique of traditional government processes, and an effort to tilt the table away from impasse.

Criticizing government for favoring the expensive achievement of non-action is hardly new, and generations of reforms have wrestled with the problem. What is intriguing about the use of mediation to address this problem is the gap between the satisfaction expressed by users of the process and the detached evaluation of it. In short, people who use it like it, but there is nearly no evidence that it works. (It is, of course, a good thing that people like the process they use, especially if the results are not worse when compared with the processes that are less soul-satisfying, but such comparison has not yet been done.)

What is true in public policy mediation is also true in the mediation of other disputes. Mediating divorce disputes, commercial disputes, and community disputes has many adherents and little that can be called hard evidence of effectiveness. So why do people continue to use mediation? Three reasons.

First, there is a great, felt need to find a better way. The costs of failure are considerable and painful. In public policy mediation, the lost money and time, and in the case of environmental problems, the lost opportunity to solve those problems, has caused a widening circle of people to feel the pain and seek a better way. Second, there is a substantial, growing, and persuasive literature, of which the present volume is a fine example, setting out the logic and techniques of the better way. From professional manuals to airport paperbacks, anyone frustrated by conflict is offered the promise of relief. And third, participants and providers generally enjoy it.

Underlying these reasons is hope. It is a hope that the use of better techniques can resolve disputes. And it is the hope that we are clever enough to get better at the devising of techniques. It is a hope that when we are immersed in some inevitable conflict, we can transcend that immersion, step outside it, and seek to solve it. (In the humbler version, we only manage the conflict.) It is a hope that the stimulus of conflict, when managed appropriately, can lead to creativity, to solutions that were not apparent before the process of resolution began, solutions which satisfy the parties more deeply than would a more traditional approach to the conflict. It is, in short, the hope that we can be better people than much of our history might suggest.

None of these hopes is based on much evidence, which is why they are hopes and not predictions. What is striking, however, is how powerful these hopes are. The field of dispute resolution continues to grow and thrive; the subfield of mediation adds practitioners and supporters on a daily basis; and the specialized niche of public policy mediation seems solidly placed.

This is a book by a psychologist and a lawyer. Their commitment to the environment led them into the thickets of complex disputing, and their frustration in those thickets led them to mediation. This is a common career path: from traditional vocation to a problem defined as conflict, to mediation. Poitras and Renaud have now gone the additional step. They have written a book of admirable clarity that lays out one basic set of understandings of the field, including the techniques and rationale that tell how to do the job better. Not everyone chooses to write a book, but a by-product of hope is the impulse to tug at the public sleeve, to tell the world that over here is a better path.

Hope is what keeps this field going. It is the hope of the parties, of the government, and of the mediators. It is an honorable hope with admirable goals. This book is well calculated to help many reach those goals.

David Matz
Professor of Law
Director, Graduate Programs in Dispute Resolution
University of Massachusetts, Boston

FOREWORD
TO THE FRENCH EDITION

Today's society continues to turn to the courts and administrative tribunals to resolve disputes in all sectors of activity. Yet, in the past decade, countless reports dealing with the magistrature, government and legal profession have highlighted the problems inherent in our judicial system. There is widespread consensus on the premise that we must find more creative ways of handling conflict and that litigation should be a last resort.

I have spent the past five years helping government adopt more flexible dispute resolution methods. During this time, I have seen a move towards alternative means of managing conflict, particularly in the context of family, commercial and correctional services disputes. I have also seen the government invest considerable time and energy in having its agencies and officials employ alternative dispute resolution techniques in-house. The next step will undoubtedly be to apply these new approaches to multiparty disputes between government, industry and individuals.

This book is highly relevant, given the fact that mediation is one such alternative to traditional dispute resolution methods.

The value of mediation has been discussed at length in recent years. It makes disputing parties part of the settlement process and allows them to discuss the problem in a setting that is conducive to openly voicing their needs and identifying common interests and areas of disagreement. A neutral party, or mediator, helps the disputants work together to find a solution that serves the interests of all involved.

In this volume, Jean Poitras and Pierre Renaud present an excellent, unprecedented reflective study, which is both well-balanced and systematic, on mediation's potential for reconciling interests in public disputes. The authors combine theory, practice and concrete examples to demonstrate the advantages of mediation as a means of reconciling interests. A compendium of useful ideas, the volume is intended as much for experienced readers as for anyone interested in learning more about public or private-sector dispute resolution.

Drawing from their own experience, the authors clearly explain the different phases and dynamics of the mediation process and their usefulness for reconciling interests in public disputes.

No public agency or body should be without this book. Until recently, mediation was rarely called into service as a means for approaching and settling public disputes. Yet, the use of mediation to identify common interests demonstrates open-mindedness and, above all, confirms the responsibility of our decision-makers and administrators to do all they can to resolve the many situations of conflict that arise within our society.

Guy Baron
Attorney
Justice Canada
Ottawa

Introduction

INTRODUCTION

Social conflicts are part of everyday life. It would be utopian to think that countries with millions of inhabitants could go forever without any sort of conflict arising. We all have different interests, and every public project or policy, be it local or national in scope, impacts directly or indirectly on those interests. Similarly, a dispute which is initially private may become public if it extends beyond the immediate parties.

Public disputes generally involve the use of public resources: highways, social programs, even ecosystems. One of the characteristics of public resources is that they are accessible and directly or indirectly benefit a large segment of the population.

Trying to balance the interests of parties divided over a given project or policy is a formidable task, given the wide range of interests involved. It is therefore natural that some decisions be considered biased enough to generate conflict between groups with competing interests. In this respect, conflict is a sign of imbalance.

The aim of this book is not to determine whether conflicts are good or bad for society since they are inevitable, but rather to explore how public disputes can be resolved, or how greater balance between the interests of all parties can be achieved. Achieving efficient, fair conflict management is the very essence of this volume.

Traditional methods for resolving public disputes involving several interest groups consist in ruling in favour of one side. A construction permit for a landfill site is granted with or without conditions, or is denied outright. A public policy is either approved and implemented, or rejected out of hand. Public officials can choose from among various forums (the courts, public hearings, referendums, etc.) to settle the conflicts arising from these decisions. However, such forums tend to create or sustain an adversarial relationship between disputing parties. Rarely do they seek a mutually satisfactory outcome, since their purpose is to determine which proposed solution will dominate.

Consequently, despite the fact that there are many decision-making authorities mandated to rule democratically on public sector disputes, there are unfortunately few social means for resolving such disputes. Ruling, or rendering a "verdict", connotes favouring one party over another; resolving a dispute means finding a solution that reconciles parties' divergent interests. Why not sit the disputants down and allow them to negotiate their own mutually acceptable solution? This method consists in arriving at a settlement that balances the different interests through negotiation. In theory, parties should continue negotiating until they reach a settlement that satisfies as many interests as possible, at which point a natural balance will be reached. However, for this to happen, negotiations must be productive and the parties must gradually move towards an agreement that maximizes mutual gain. Unfortunately, this is not usually the case when parties are left to negotiate on their own.

Framing[1] negotiations is critical for arriving at a balanced solution that reflects the interests of all parties. In this sense, mediation is a valuable tool, because it is a process in which a neutral party specializing in negotiation and group dynamics assists the disputants in their search for a settlement. Among other things, mediation facilitates face-to-face discussion and favours reconciliation of interests. It is also a consensual approach to conflict management that fosters coordinated effort and productive exchange. For all these reasons, it is important that public and private sector administrators, organizational leaders and citizens be familiar with the fundamentals of the mediation process.

This book combines theory and practice to explain the procedure for reconciling interests in public disputes. Chapter 1 discusses the nature of conflict, the attendant social costs and benefits, and conflict management models. Chapter 2 explains the conceptual principles of mediation and discusses types of disputes that benefit from mediation. The remaining chapters deal with the substance of mediation as applied to public disputes. More specifically, Chapter 3

---

1 In this book, "framing" means structuring, or establishing the framework for, and supervising the negotiation process.

discusses the mediator's role as manager of the dispute resolution process, while Chapter 4 explains the process used by the mediator to help parties reconcile their interests and work together to find a solution. Chapter 5 discusses how to change the dynamics of the negotiation process in order to preempt conflict escalation and encourage the parties to collaborate. Chapter 6 looks at how mediation can be applied in public disputes, focusing on ethics and transparency. The aim of this book is therefore to provide the reader with an overview of mediation as a means for reconciling divergent interests in a public dispute.

Chapter 1

A New Means of Managing Public Disputes

CHAPTER 1

A NEW MEANS OF MANAGING PUBLIC DISPUTES

1.1 THE NATURE OF CONFLICT

In its nature, a conflict involves opposition. For instance, a group of industrialists and environmentalists may battle over the level of water pollution caused by a proposed plant because they disagree on the receiving environment's capacity to dissolve pollutants. Citizens groups and a municipality may be at loggerheads over a local development policy because they advocate different land use plans. Two interest groups could be at odds over the construction of a new highway, each advocating a different route. Each of these examples involves opposing interests or opposing means. Different interest groups are likely to have different priorities or different ways of doing things. This opposition generates conflict.

The dynamics of a conflict situation are determined by the issues underlying the opposition, i.e. conflicting interests or conflicting means for satisfying a common or shared interest.[2] An example of conflicting interests might be when a municipality and a citizens group are divided over the pending construction of a bridge. The city may wish to achieve a road access, while the citizens may want to prevent visual and noise pollution. An example of disagreement over the means for satisfying a common interest might be two interest groups

---

2 For a more in-depth analysis of this concept, see *The Resolution of Conflict: Constructive and Destructive Processes* by M. Deutsch.

that are fighting over the appropriate development and size of a public parking lot. While both groups may recognize the need for a parking lot, each would like to see its own proposal prevail. Opposition alone is therefore not enough to determine the nature of a conflict; the dynamics of the conflict must also be identified, i.e. whether it stems from conflicting interests or conflicting means.

Furthermore, additional factors may transform the initial dynamics. A group may feel frustrated and publicly blame another group and its project. Boycotts, demonstrations or strikes may be organized to protest a specific project or policy. All of these factors can render a conflict situation much more complex and more difficult to resolve, causing the conflict to escalate and intensify.[3] The nature of a conflict, therefore, depends on both opposition and escalation.

1.1.1   Opposition

Without opposition, there would be no conflict. When parties have different goals and their means to achieve them do not intersect, there is little risk of confrontation. It is when goals and means are incompatible that conflict is likely to emerge. For instance, players (individuals, groups, organizations or nations) may not want the same thing, in which case they may have differing interests, goals, even values. A municipality may propose building a shopping centre, while a group of citizens may want to preserve the city's rural character. The municipality's economic interests therefore clash with the social interests of those citizens.

While disputing parties may share complementary interests or goals, they may disagree on the means for achieving these goals, for example, on the conception of a project or a policy, or on a deadline. A municipality and citizens groups may agree on the importance of linking the city to a commuter rail system, but be divided over the site or design of the train station. This is a case of conflicting means, or disagreement over the "how" of a project or policy. Figure 1 illustrates the two possible conflict dynamics.

---

3 The notion of additional conflict is explored in *The Function of Social Conflict* by L. Coser.

FIGURE 1

Conflict dynamics

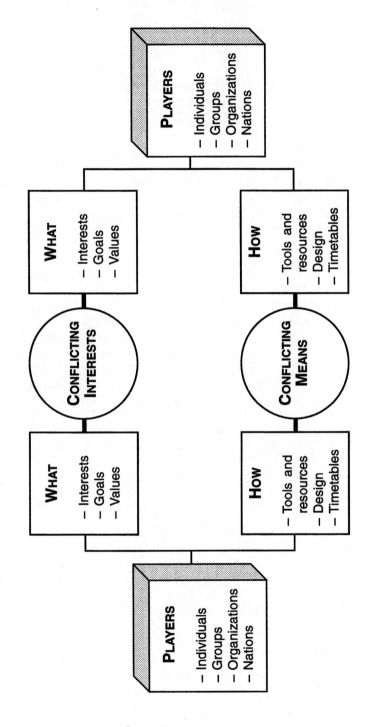

1.1.1.1   Conflicting interests

The first dynamic of opposition has to do with diverging interests. In a public dispute, the interests at stake can be broken down into three categories:[4] economic, environmental and social (Figure 2). Job creation and a project's financial profitability are examples of economic interests, while cleaning up a polluted river or protecting a natural site are examples of environmental interests. Social interests generally entail ensuring citizens' quality of life and meeting community needs. All three categories are associated with a given political context, which can influence the predominance of one interest over another. In a political context marked by restraint and economic recession, for example, economic and social interests are likely to prevail over environmental interests. Figure 2 summarizes the interests at stake in a public conflict.

For any given project or policy, certain groups will tend to promote economic interests, while others will be more concerned about the environment. Individual interests depend on the use the group makes or intends to make of public property.[5] For instance, developers will be more sensitive to economic interests, whereas environmental groups will be more concerned with environmental interests, and citizens, about protecting their quality of life, or social interests. These different priorities are the bases of disputes involving conflicting interests. Reconciling those interests is the goal of dispute resolution.

---

4 For more on this concept, see *Définir les rapports entre l'évaluation environnementale et le développement durable : la clé de l'avenir* by B. Sadler and P. Jacobs.
5 See *Estuarine Quality Use and Public Perception* by N. West.

FIGURE 2

Aspects of a public dispute

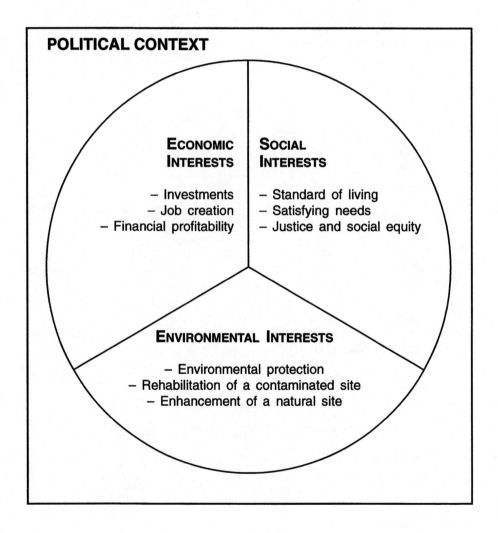

1.1.1.2   Conflicting means

The second type of dynamic opposition involves disagreement over the means used to achieve a common goal. For example, disputing parties may disagree over the alignment of a new highway, the design of a new convention centre, or the timetable for implementing a new policy. The parties share a common interest in that they all want the proposed highway, convention centre or policy, but they disagree on how the project or policy is to be enacted. The resolution of disputes involving conflicting means focuses on coordinating party efforts. Case dynamics help to determine the strategy used for its resolution.

1.1.2   Conflict escalation

As mentioned above, opposition alone does not determine the nature of a conflict. In fact, various factors may cause an existing conflict to escalate. The disputants may regularly make inflammatory public statements, or the dispute may be aggravated by personality conflicts between the members or heads of an organization. Conflicts can also become more heated due to poor dissemination of information. Everyday occurrences regularly show just how important these factors can become in public disputes. The most common reasons for conflict escalation are disagreement over scientific data, unhealthy psychological relationships and differing values.[6] When analyzing a public dispute, it is important to be aware of possible sources of escalation, as they often fan the flames of conflict and hinder joint problem-solving.

1.2   SOCIAL COSTS AND BENEFITS OF CONFLICT

Why is dispute resolution so important? For one thing, because disputes are costly for both individuals and society as a whole. A transportation strike can paralyze an entire city. The costs of delaying a project can be staggering. A dispute over a government policy can hinder economic growth. Conflict resolution saves money, but also

---

6 For examples of sources of escalation, see *The Mediation Process: Practical Strategies for Resolving Conflict* by C.W. Moore.

plays an important social role[7] insofar as it fosters change, adaptation and progress. Dispute resolution can lead to new situations or new arrangements that are better adapted to individual and societal needs. A social cost/benefit analysis is aimed at weighing the social costs of a dispute and the social benefits. The lower the cost and the greater the benefits, the more a public dispute is likely to result in social progress. Cost/benefit analysis of a conflict is important for it highlights the advantages of efficient conflict management.

1.2.1   Social costs of confrontation

Disputes over such things as development projects, regulations and government policies are generally very expensive, not just for the parties directly involved, but for the general public as well. Direct social costs obviously include a considerable loss of time, money and opportunity. The indirect social costs of confrontation include social stress, destroyed partnerships and social impasse, all of which have major repercussions.

1.2.1.1   Economic losses

The most direct cost of conflict is clearly the attendant economic losses. In the case of a cancelled project, for example, both the developer and the communities which may have benefited from the project suffer a direct economic blow. Where a project is proposed without attempting to find an alternative that serves the interests of all parties, there is also opportunity loss, since it may have been possible to do more or better for the same investment, or with another, more appropriate, project altogether. Conflict can result in considerable indirect economic losses as well. For instance, during the Canadian-Spanish dispute over fishing off the Grand Banks of Newfoundland, Spain retaliated by cancelling or delaying a number of trade agreements with Canada. This constitutes an indirect economic loss, because the agreements had nothing to do with the original dispute.

---

7 Notion developed in *The Function of Social Conflict* by L. Coser.

1.2.1.2   Social stress

A major indirect cost generally associated with public disputes is increased stress, both social stress, which includes tension between the antagonists, and stress experienced by citizens affected by the dispute. For example, when demonstrators put up a roadblock, they may limit public access to resources or a major facility. In this sense, public disputes can affect a large segment of the population and end up requiring enactment of special legislation, as is often the case in public transportation, airline, shipping or railway disputes. These are all situations where citizens may undergo intense stress. A protracted dispute can be a major strain not only on the immediate parties, but on the whole population as well.

1.2.1.3   Destroyed partnerships

Today, partnerships are vital to development. The different levels of government no longer have the economic resources to finance development projects on their own; in fact, federal and provincial governments, cities and the private sector are forming more part-nerships than ever. Politically, citizens want increasing involvement in the decision-making process, while in terms of the environment, there is less and less tolerance for projects with potentially adverse effects that are implemented without a hearing allowing the public to voice its concerns. Partnerships have thus become an integral part of all projects. Unfortunately, the bad blood created during a dispute can destroy any possibility of future cooperation between the groups involved. This can be a long-term side-effect of poorly managed con-flict.

1.2.1.4   Social impasse

A paradox exists in our society: despite the common desire for positive change, confrontation between interest groups leads to the contrary, paralysis.[8] Public disputes regularly result in project can-cellation or undue decision-making delays. For example, the environment is interesting in that regard. The "economic-develop-ment-at-any-cost" mentality of the early 1900s had a devastating effect on the environment, causing widespread ecosystem degrada-

---

8 See *Breaking the Impasse: Consensual Approaches to Resolving Public Disputes* by L. Susskind and J. Cruikshank.

tion. On the other hand, systematically questioning the environmental impact of all new projects has weakened the economic fabric of certain regions. We face a situation in which meeting the economic interests of the population interferes with environmental interests and vice versa. We are at an impasse, despite the common will to achieve integrated development.

1.2.2   Social benefits of collaboration

Despite considerable social cost, conflict is the driving force of social change and thus has a social value. Depending on the situation, conflict can generate four kinds of social benefits: integrative solutions, reconciliation of interests, intergroup cooperation and social evolution. Analyzing the potential benefits of public disputes is vital, as it highlights the advantages of choosing a resolution process that minimizes costs and maximizes social gains. Figure 3 summarizes the social costs/benefits of public disputes.

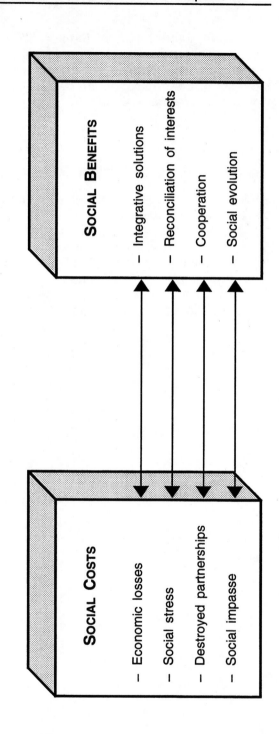

FIGURE 3

The two aspects of public disputes

1.2.2.1 Integrative solutions

A consensual approach aimed at satisfying diverging interests has the advantage of generating integrative solutions, i.e. solutions that satisfy the interests of the entire population as opposed to those of a single group. A provincial road construction project could be carried out in conjunction with a municipal bicycle path development project. Instead of fighting over land use, the two levels of government could work together, combining their respective projects to create new opportunities and even reduce building costs. This approach is much more integrative than simply dividing the land among the two projects. At the same time, it maximizes social gain.

1.2.2.2 Reconciliation of interests

Public disputes may also be beneficial if they result in the interests of several players being reconciled. Conflict serves to identify interests that were neglected in the preliminary versions of a project, policy, or other. A project developed by a single group, a developer for instance, will likely neglect or underevaluate interests of importance to another group, i.e. environmental and social considerations, due to a lack of knowledge or understanding. In this respect, disputes bring into focus interests which have been overlooked in the initial proposal.

However, it is not enough to just realize that interests have been overlooked; those interests must be addressed in the dispute resolution process. Traditional approaches to dispute resolution tend to deny the legitimacy of new interests, which precludes a mutual-gain outcome, let alone interparty cooperation. Conflict only has social benefits when it is handled so as to use these new interests to enhance projects, regulations or public policies. The most effective way to reconcile interests is to explore each option and determine how it can be incorporated into the initial proposal. Various versions of a project can be studied in order to find a solution that satisfies as many interests as possible.

1.2.2.3 Interparty cooperation

Paradoxically, conflict can also bring people closer together. While it is true that a dispute generally creates resentment between the opponents, an innovative solution that satisfies all parties can encourage project developers, interest groups and citizens groups to

17

collaborate. Feeling involved in the decision-making process fosters more lasting ties between the various social groups. In this sense, conflict management that respects the interests of each party and seeks a creative resolution can encourage greater interparty cooperation. Handled properly, disputes can bring people together and, consequently, yield greater social benefits.

1.2.2.4   Social evolution

Conflict may lead to other social benefits such as change. Innovative solutions created following a dispute can become tomorrow's standards. For instance, the use of tree-planted hillocks to reduce the visual impact of electric generating stations is now common practice. Had there never been any conflict over the visual and environmental impact of these stations, their design never would have evolved. Conflict therefore provides an impetus for social change, evolution of public resource management and positive interaction between social groups, all of which generate long-term benefits.

1.3   EFFICIENT CONFLICT MANAGEMENT

According to cost/benefit analysis principles, efficient conflict management should minimize costs while maximizing social benefits. Conflict management methods that comply with this principle are considered collaborative approaches to dispute resolution, as they focus on maximizing the social benefits of cooperation. In contrast, adversarial approaches unintentionally maximize the social costs of confrontation. These two approaches are at opposite ends of the conflict management spectrum, with the various techniques used to handle disputes somewhere in between.

Parliamentary commissions, public hearings and judicial litigation are all adversarial approaches to conflict management. At the other end of the spectrum are so-called alternative, collaborative approaches: partnership, assisted negotiation, conciliation and particularly mediation. The two poles of the conflict management paradigm can be compared on the basis of four main features: first, the discussion level and the axis of reflection; second, the decision level and the axis of solutions. Table 1 compares the two paradigms around these four main features.

TABLE 1

Comparison of adversarial and collaborative approaches to conflict management

FEATURES	ADVERSARIAL APPROACHES	COLLABORATIVE APPROACHES
Level of discussion	Indirect communication	Direct communication
Axis of reflection	Argumentation	Problem-solving
Level of decision	Independant decision-maker	Consensual
Axis of solutions	Win-lose outcome	Win-win outcome

1.3.1   Level of discussion

Adversarial conflict management processes are based on indirect interaction between parties. In court, for example, the disputants "talk" through their lawyers. In a public hearing, the promoters and opponents of a project do not engage in face-to-face discussion, but rather tell their concerns to a commissioner who then makes suggestions and recommendations. At the government level, citizens are generally able to participate only indirectly in the decision-making process by lobbying their local member of parliament. Discussion based on indirect communication leaves little room for consensual solutions, since the disputing parties never have the opportunity to discuss their respective needs and concerns face to face. This aspect of adversarial conflict management hampers the reconciliation of interests and cooperation between parties.

Reconciling diverging interests requires direct interparty communication. After all, who understands a group's interests better than the group itself? And who is better placed to compromise on those interests than the group concerned? How can parties become partners if there is no face-to-face interaction? Only two-way communication makes it possible to develop a cooperative relationship, which, in turn, fosters mutual understanding of interests and enables common goals to be identified. Collaborative approaches to conflict management are predicated on face-to-face negotiation.

1.3.2   Axis of reflexion

Another important comparative feature of adversarial and collaborative conflict management methods is the axis of reflexion. Adversarial approaches lean towards argumentation. Rather than attempting to identify the source of the problem and find the best possible solution, negotiations are aimed at determining who is right. Each party pleads its case by trying to discredit the other's proposals. Discussion based on argumentation clearly discourages the reconciliation of interests and integrative solutions. Furthermore, the possibility of interparty cooperation is virtually inexistant.

In contrast, collaborative approaches target side-by-side problem-solving. The aim of negotiations is not for one party to impose its interests on the other party or parties, but to find common ground and devise a solution that is acceptable to all parties. The goal is to enhance the initial project so that everyone gains. When negotiations are aimed at resolving the problem, it is no longer a matter of determining who is right or who wins, but rather of which solution produces the most winners. Because they target joint problem-solving, collaborative approaches are more effective in reconciling interests in public disputes.

1.3.3   Level of decision

The main difference between adversarial and collaborative conflict management where decision-making is concerned lies in who makes the final decision. With adversarial approaches, a third party generally rules in favour of one side. A commissioner, for example, examines the opinions and briefs submitted by the disputants and then makes a recommendation to the minister, who hands down the final ruling. A judge or arbitrator listens to the arguments of party representatives and then renders a "verdict". With approaches that rely on third-party decision-makers, the actual parties in conflict have no say in its resolution.

Collaborative approaches, on the other hand, are based on consensus building. Parties work together to develop mutually acceptable solutions. For there to be agreement, the solution must satisfy all parties. By giving parties a say in the final outcome and allowing them to participate in the settlement process, consensual dispute resolution is more apt to generate solutions that reconcile interests and maximize mutual gain. Consensual approaches empower parties to share in decision-making and determine their own dispute resolution.[9] In fact, where the parties are unable to reach an agreement, the mediator does not settle the matter for them like a judge or arbitrator, and the dispute remains, for the time, unresolved. Decisions are made according to the parties' needs and rythm of decision-making.

1.3.4   Axis of solutions

The cumulative effect of these differences in the type of discussion, axis of reflection and decision-making process between

---

9 See the article by R. Baruch Bush, *Efficiency and Protection or Empowerment and Recognition: The Mediator's Role and Ethical Standards in Mediation.*

adversarial and collaborative approaches is manifest in the types of solutions they generate. Adversarial approaches tend to produce "win-lose" outcomes. Thanks to its strong arguments, one of the parties will have succeeded in convincing an independent decision-maker to rule in its favour. Collaborative approaches, on the other hand, tend to foster "win-win" solutions.

Win-win solutions are not a philosophical fantasy. They are the logical consequence of the reconciliation of interests. Diverging interests can only be reconciled, however, through face-to-face negotiation. Parties work collaboratively to resolve the dispute and reach a consensual decision on the best possible option. Since it is unlikely that a party will support a solution that puts it at a disadvantage, there will not be consensus unless there is mutual gain, which is why consensual dispute resolution processes generate "win-win" outcomes.

1.4   MEDIATION: A COLLABORATIVE APPROACH

Although several collaborative conflict management techniques exist, we feel mediation is the most effective. The mediation process can best be described using an analogy. Imagine two children arguing. Their first reaction is to go running to their parents to have them decide who's right. If the children are very young, the parents will solve the problem by imposing a solution, e.g. "Let your brother play with your toy." As the children develop social skills, they can be taught more collaborative ways of resolving their differences. Instead of settling the issue for them, parents can help their children negotiate a solution. The children can then trade and play with each other's toys because they want to, not because they are told to.

Although mediating a public dispute is obviously much more complex, it is also based on the principle of negotiation. Mediation is a dispute resolution process in which a non-partisan mediator helps the disputants resolve the conflict through a joint effort. It empowers parties by encouraging them to engage in face-to-face discussion. The mediator keeps the parties focused on solving the problem, and decisions are consensual. Mediation also allows communities to play an active role in projects that affect them and enhances their ability to find imaginative solutions to social conflicts.[10] Making them part

---

10 Concept primarily developed in *Public Conflict Resolution: A Transformative Approach* by F. Dukes.

of the solution generally benefits all parties. This is why mediation is considered a collaborative conflict management technique.

1.5 SUMMARY

In this chapter, we have defined the nature of public disputes in terms of opposition and escalation. First, disputes result from opposing public interests (economic, environmental and social). Conflict dynamics differ depending on whether the disagreement arises from diverging interests or differing views on the means for satisfying a common interest. Second, disputes often escalate, making the conflict more adversarial. The social costs of conflict generally include a reduced quality of life, less cooperation between social groups, and fewer economic and social development projects. However, conflict can also generate social benefits, such as change and renewal. In short, social conflict is a fact of life, and efficient resolution can both reduce costs and generate major social benefits.

The analysis in this chapter highlights the importance of efficient conflict management. Unresolved disputes can lead to needless costs, and dispute resolution that does not seek the best possible solution leads to fewer social gains. Unlike adversarial approaches to conflict management, i.e. most traditional methods, collaborative approaches promote an integrative outcome that maximizes mutual gain. Collaborative conflict management is characterized by face-to-face negotiations that focus on problem-solving, consensus-building and win-win solutions. One such approach is mediation, which is discussed in further detail in the next chapter.

Chapter 2

Mediation: Concept and Model

CHAPTER 2

MEDIATION: CONCEPT AND MODEL

2.1   THE MEDIATION CONCEPT

In the previous chapter, we looked at the need to move from adversarial models for managing public disputes to collaborative models that target the reconciliation of interests. However, this shift cannot take place overnight and outside assistance to help and guide the disputants may be advisable, even necessary, to avoid the numerous potential pitfalls along the way. In this regard, mediation is an excellent collaborative dispute resolution technique.

But what exactly is mediation? Basically, it can be defined as a process in which an impartial third party, or mediator, helps the disputants negotiate their own agreement. At the negotiating stage, the disputants work together to find a solution that meets their mutual and respective needs. Before exploring any further into the mediation process and dynamics, we need to take a closer look at the concept of mediation in the context of public disputes: What are the underlying principles? How is mediation applied to public disputes? What are the minimum conditions required for mediation to be constructive? This chapter attempts to answer these basic questions in order to provide an overview of the process.

2.2 THE CONCEPTUAL BASES OF MEDIATION

Mediation is a dispute resolution and management process whose conceptual structure is based on the notions of the social costs and benefits inherent in conflict developed in Chapter 1. As a management method, mediation seeks to minimize the costs of conflict while maximizing the benefits. Given that most of these costs are incurred as a result of confrontation between parties and that the possible benefits derive from interparty cooperation, it is reasonable to assume that the efficiency of a conflict management process such as mediation is proportional to the degree of confrontation and cooperation. Where there is extensive cooperation and little confrontation, there will be maximum efficiency. The efficiency of the mediation process can be expressed using the following equation.

Equation 1: Efficiency = Cooperation — Confrontation

This simple equation shows efficiency as a function of interparty cooperation and confrontation. The goal of mediation is to resolve the dispute by reducing confrontation and increasing cooperation. Where cooperation is greater than confrontation, the process will be efficient and the dispute settled. Where confrontation outweighs cooperation, the process will be inefficient and the conflict will escalate. An inefficient dispute resolution generally leads to a conflict spiral.[11] The parties can choose between getting caught up in the dispute (inefficient, negative outcome) or disentangling themselves from the conflict spiral to find a solution (efficient, positive outcome).

As a conflict management process, mediation seeks to tip the scales in favour of cooperation, as opposed to confrontation, to ensure an efficient process that results in agreement. The purpose of the mediator's intervention is two-fold: to reduce confrontation and increase cooperation between the parties. To understand this aspect, we need to expand upon the notions of confrontation and cooperation.

Confrontation can be defined in practical terms using the everyday example of a couple with only one car. It's Saturday night and the husband wants the car to go meet his friends at the casino. His wife wants to go to the movies with her sister. This is a case in which differing interests create a problem. The farther apart those interests are, the greater the confrontation. If the husband and wife both wanted to go to the movies, but to see different films, there would likely be less confrontation. The first element of confrontation is there-

---

11 For a detailed explanation of this concept, see *Social Conflict: Escalation, Stalemate and Settlement* by D. Pruitt and J. Rubin.

fore a difference of interest, with the degree of confrontation being proportional to how far apart those interests are.

Continuing with the example of our stereotyped couple, suppose the wife feels she has been wronged and accuses her husband of being selfish and caring only about going out and spending money with his friends. Her husband gets upset and claims that he pays for most of the car-related expenses and should be able to use it whenever he wants. Right away, we can see that the conflict has just escalated a notch. However, the original problem, i.e. who gets to use the car, is still the same. Conflicts escalate for any number of reasons, from psychological factors to lawsuits to armed warfare.

The elements of confrontation as illustrated in the above example can be expressed using the following equation.

Equation 2: Confrontation = Differing interests + Escalation

In reducing confrontation, mediation seeks to narrow the difference in interests and, where possible, eliminate sources of escalation. Reconciling interests entails identifying and resolving the issues underlying the conflict. Mediation helps the parties discover another way of achieving their respective goals without necessarily sacrificing their interests. Going back to our couple, the wife could drop her husband off at the casino on her way to the movies and then neither would have to concede their interests. However, in order to reduce confrontation, the psychological, legal, political or other aspects of the dispute sometimes have to be "deflated" before any attempt can be made to compensate interests. It is unlikely that our couple will solve their car problem as long as they continue to attack and blame each other. In order to reduce confrontation in public disputes, the mediator's actions must be directed at reconciling interests while "deflating" the conflict.

Cooperation can also be defined in practical terms using the example of weekly housecleaning. Let's say you have a two-bedroom apartment that you have to clean alone; this normally takes you two hours. A friend offers to help. Since there is twice the manpower, it is logical to assume that the job will get done in half the time, your efforts and your friend's will combine to increase efficiency.

One of the first elements of cooperation is the combined action of two or more parties.[12] However, as we all know, working with

---

12 See *The Resolution of Conflict: Constructive and Destructive Processes* by M. Deutsch.

someone else does not necessarily guarantee greater efficiency. You also need motivation. For example, if having two people do the housework means that you can finish earlier so you can go to the movies, there is likely to be greater collaboration. It will be completely different, however, if after you have finished the housework, you have to do something uninteresting like your income tax return. Motivation is an important factor in cooperation. The notion of cooperation can be expressed using the following equation.

Equation 3: Cooperation = Sum of actions + Motivation

Unfortunately, the key element of cooperation, i.e. sum of actions, is not automatic. For the two people in our example to clean the same part of a room would likely be a waste of time. The parties' efforts must be coordinated for their collaboration to be efficient. Consequently, one mediation strategy is to coordinate party efforts in order to achieve a common goal. Motivation, for its part, is related to the notion of shared interest. If parties find they have more to gain by working together, there will be more of an incentive to do so. Another strategy used in mediation consists in taking a mutual-gain approach in order to encourage interparty cooperation. Figure 4 summarizes the overall equation for efficient conflict management and the conceptual principles of mediation.

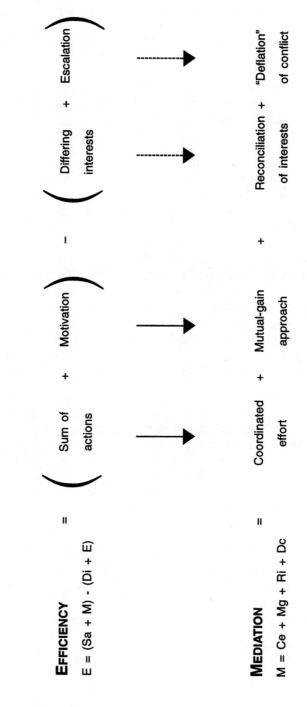

FIGURE 4

Mediation model and concept

EFFICIENCY =

E = (Sa + M) - (Di + E)

MEDIATION =

M = Ce + Mg + Ri + Dc

31

2.3   MEDIATION IN THE CONTEXT OF PUBLIC DISPUTES

The fundamentals of mediation expounded in the previous section are not unique to personal disputes, but are also applicable to public disputes. Public disputes involve the same elements of confrontation and cooperation, and require the same intervention. Although the parties to a public dispute are generally groups rather than individuals, efficient management using mediation is based on the same principles as mediation of personal disputes.

As in personal disputes, confrontation in public disputes stems from differing interests and conflict escalation. A city may want to build a bridge over a river in order to develop an industrial zone, while residents living on the banks of the river see the bridge as a threat to their quality of life. A promoter may wish to incinerate sewage sludge, whereas environmentalists would rather see it reclaimed. Large-scale agricultural projects may anger citizens, who lobby their municipal council. The council might declare a moratorium on the project, leading to frustration among farmers. These are just a few cases in which opposing interests can turn into a public dispute. The conflict can escalate when groups demonstrate on Parliament Hill, take their case to court or engage in mudslinging through the newspapers. The same elements of confrontation are found in public disputes; in fact, they may even be magnified.

The same elements of cooperation are also present in public disputes. Cooperation is absent from disputes that cannot be resolved. Usually, there is also minimum coordination of the contending parties' efforts: construction goes ahead before a final decision is rendered, which could mean considerable losses should the project not be accepted. Furthermore, there is generally little incentive for the disputing parties to cooperate and no attempt is made to maximize benefits. Considerable economies of scale are foregone because neighbouring cities and citizens groups remain deadlocked. On the other hand, when cooperation flourishes, it can produce astonishing results. The city of Malden, Massachusetts, successfully used mediation to hammer out an agreement between the municipal government, the Chamber of commerce and citizens on recommendations for balancing city revenues and expenditures, thereby avoiding arbitrary cutbacks and preempting conflict.[13] This is a good

---

13 For a detailed explanation of the Malden case, see *New Approaches to Resolving Local Public Disputes* by D. Madigan *et al.*

example of how mediation can be used to both maximize gain and minimize loss.[14]

Since public disputes entail the same elements as other types of conflict, the same guiding principles apply to their resolution. The aim of mediation is to prevent the conflict from escalating, reconcile interests, determine a mutual-gain solution, and coordinate party efforts. These four principles form the basis of public mediation, which may be defined as a process in which a non-partisan facilitator assists the parties in finding a way to reconcile their interests through a joint effort by "deflating" possible sources of conflict and identifying common interests.

It is interesting to note that mediation as defined above is compatible with the principles of sustainable development. Reconciling interests enables further integration of different community interests, thereby fostering solutions that are endorsed by all parties. Furthermore, since mediation encourages coordinated effort and a resolution that maximizes mutual gain, it also encourages parties to cooperate and work as partners. Finally, the combination of reconciliation of interests, cooperation and partnership fosters integrative solutions. In this sense, mediation embraces three fundamental principles of sustainable development, making it an even better tool for managing public disputes.

2.4   PREREQUISITES FOR SUCCESSFUL MEDIATION

Psychologists often describe psychotherapy using the following anecdote: "How many psychologists does it take to change a light bulb? Just one, but the light bulb has to want to change...." Humour notwithstanding, this anecdote voices a truth that could easily be applied to mediation. The mediator can only apply the four principles of mediation if the parties are willing to resolve the dispute. This willingness is the most fundamental prerequisite for successful mediation.[15] More specifically, four prerequisites are required for mediation

---

14 For other examples of mediated disputes resulting in the reconciliation of interests, maximum gain and minimum loss, see *La médiation et les conflits entourant les projets d'infrastructures routières* by P. Renaud.

15 In *Mediation: A Comprehensive Guide to Resolving Conflicts Without Litigation*, J. Folberg and A. Taylor propose criteria for determining whether mediation would be helpful in resolving private disputes.

to be productive: willingness to resolve the dispute, willingness to explore areas of disagreement, willingness to seek a win-win outcome, and authority to make decisions. Table 2 illustrates the interaction between the principles of and prerequisites for successful mediation.

TABLE 2

Interaction between the principles of and prerequisites for successful mediation

PRINCIPLES OF MEDIATION	PREREQUISITES
Prevent conflict from escalating	Willingness to resolve the dispute
Reconcile interests	Willingness to explore areas of disagreement
Seek a mutual-gain solution	Willingness to seek a win-win outcome
Coordinate party effort	Authority to make decisions

2.4.1 Willingness to resolve the dispute

The prime condition for engaging in mediation is clearly the parties' willingness to negotiate. However, a distinction must be made between wanting to negotiate and wanting to win. You may want to resolve a dispute by negotiating a solution, or you may want to resolve it by eliminating your opponent. There needs to be an honest desire on the part of the parties to solve the problem, and to prevent the conflict from escalating. Consequently, the parties must be willing to address the situation and separate the people from the problem.[16] This does not mean that the parties must no longer feel any anger when they come to the negotiating table. It means they must recognize that hostilities need to be diminished before they can attack the source of the conflict.

2.4.2 Willingness to explore areas of disagreement

In order to reconcile interests, the disputants must be willing to identify areas of disagreement. A party may feel that the conflict exists because the other parties have misunderstood its point of view. Consequently, it may mistakenly assume that if the other parties understood the reasons for its actions, they would think the same way it does. It is easy to imagine that if all parties come to the negotiating table with this mind-set, there is little hope of success. The parties must recognize that they have differing interests and that those interests must be explored before they can be reconciled. This helps move the negotiation from a focus on positions to a focus on the interests behind those positions.[17]

2.4.3 Willingness to seek a win-win outcome

Mediation is a consensual approach to decision-making. In other words, a solution must be supported by all parties before there is agreement. Obviously a party will not agree to a solution unless it has something to gain. A consensus will be reached only if the solution is acceptable to all parties; hence the importance of a mutual-gain approach. Furthermore, a consensual agreement is possible only if

---

16 This is one of the techniques of principled negotiation described in *Getting to YES: Negotiating Agreement Without Giving In* by R. Fisher and W.L. Ury.
17 *Ibid.*

the parties make an honest effort to resolve the conflict in a mutually beneficial manner, which is why mediation will only be successful if the parties are willing to seek a win-win outcome.

2.4.4 Authority to make decisions

There is a difference between making a decision and having the power to enforce it. We may decide that we pay too much income tax and that a thirty-percent cut is a good idea, but, unfortunately, we do not have the power to act on that decision. No matter how good the proposal, if we cannot carry through on it, it is of no practical value. Similarly, a mediated negotiation is only useful if the parties share decision-making authority. Association representatives must receive a clear mandate from the association's members. Government and municipal negotiators must have decision-making authority, and negotiators for corporations and businesses must appoint a team leader to make decisions. This does not mean that the city mayor or the company president has to be at the negotiating table, but rather that their negotiating representatives must have enough room to manoeuvre to facilitate the coordination of party effort and commit to an agreement. However, it may be entirely appropriate for a negotiator to ask for time to discuss or have his superiors approve a creative or complex solution that, due to its nature, exceeds the parameters of the original negotiation.

The four prerequisites for mediation must not be considered absolute. It is highly unlikely that they will concur at the outset of a dispute. In fact, the important thing is not so much that they exist from the beginning, but that they be put in place. One of the mediator's first tasks is to assess the situation and make sure the four prerequisites potentially exist before engaging in the actual mediation process. The presence of these prerequisites ensures a mind-set that is apt to result in productive negotiation, which greatly facilitates the mediator's job of applying the principles of mediation.

2.5 SUMMARY

Throughout this chapter, we have discussed the concept underlying mediation as a form of conflict management that reduces the costs associated with confrontation and generates the benefits arising from cooperation. Four fundamental principles have been highlighted: preventing the conflict from escalating, reconciling interests, defining a mutual-gain solution and coordinating the parties' efforts. Certain prerequisites are needed for these principles to be effectively applied, i.e. the parties' willingness to resolve the dispute, their willingness to explore areas of disagreement, their willingness to seek a win-win outcome, and their authority to make decisions. In the presence of these conditions, the principles of mediation can be successfully applied and a conflict situation can become an exercise in cooperation. When cooperation outweighs confrontation, the conflict can be managed efficiently and the dispute resolved.

This concept of mediation is consistent with the principles of collaborative conflict management discussed in Chapter 1. First, "deflating" the conflict enables face-to-face discussion. Reconciling interests changes the aim of negotiations from argumentation to problem-solving. Coordinating efforts allows parties to build an agreement based on consensus instead of relying on an outside decision-maker. And finally, when parties are motivated to work together, the end solution usually generates a win-win situation through creative conflict management. Chapter 3 examines how the mediator's role is structured around the mediation concept developed in this chapter.

Chapter 3

The Mediator's Basic Tasks

CHAPTER 3

THE MEDIATOR'S BASIC TASKS

3.1   NEUTRAL FACILITATOR

Often when we have a problem, we go to an uninvolved friend for advice, the underlying principle being that an outsider whom we trust can be more objective. This same principle applies to conflict management. The assistance of a neutral party is often necessary to take discussions from an adversarial situation to a collaborative one, not because the disputing parties are negotiating in bad faith, but simply because they are too involved, often emotionally, to be able to do it on their own.

The rest of this chapter examines the basic aspects of the mediator's role from the perspective of the general tasks, skills and attitudes required for successful dispute management. It is important to bear in mind that this analysis is based on a stereotypical description of the role of mediators. While individual mediators will have specific competencies depending on their personality, experience and area of expertise, the tasks, skills and attitudes described in this chapter are the fundamentals involved in mediating a public dispute according to the principles developed in Chapter 2.

The mediator's three main tasks will be described in relation to his role as manager of the dispute resolution process. We will then look at the skills needed to carry out these tasks effectively. Finally, we will explore the attitudes underlying successful mediation. This three-fold analysis provides a comprehensive overview of the mediator's role.

3.2   ROLE OF THE MEDIATOR

The role of the mediator can be defined in terms of the four conceptual principles of mediation described in Chapter 2. The aim of mediation is to transform an inefficient dispute resolution process (negative outcome) into an efficient one (positive outcome), with the mediator's role being broken down into specific and general tasks. Specific tasks are directly related to the concept of mediation. The mediator encourages the disputants to find a solution that reconciles the interests of all parties by helping them work cooperatively. The mediator also fosters constructive dialogue in order to diminish conflict escalation and help the parties determine a mutual-gain solution. General tasks primarily consist in overseeing negotiations, or establishing the framework for the mediation process. Figure 5 illustrates the mediator's three basic tasks in relation to the concept of mediation.

FIGURE 5

The three basic tasks of the mediator

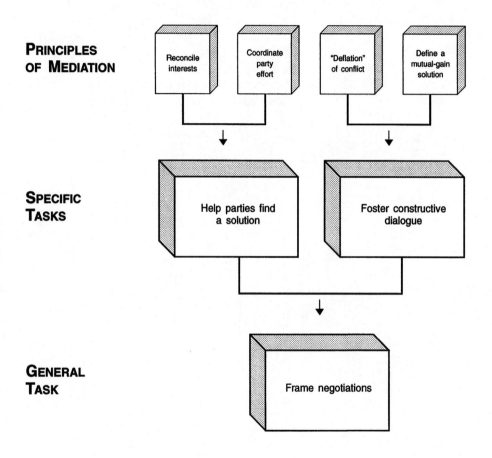

PRINCIPLES OF MEDIATION

- Reconcile interests
- Coordinate party effort
- "Deflation" of conflict
- Define a mutual-gain solution

SPECIFIC TASKS

- Help parties find a solution
- Foster constructive dialogue

GENERAL TASK

- Frame negotiations

Certain personal skills are required to carry out these basic tasks. The mediator must be able to manage the mediation process, manage interpersonal relations and solve problems. While technical expertise in the area of conflict (e.g. law, architecture, labour, environment, psychology) may also be important in specific cases, it is not mandatory.[18] In fact, it is often considered a complementary skill.

In addition to the basic competencies, the mediator must have certain natural traits. He or she must be diplomatic, have a proactive attitude and show leadership. These qualities will create a dynamic, positive setting for open, honest negotiation. Diplomacy, a proactive attitude and leadership relate to the "know how to be" of the mediator's role. Table 3 summarizes the correlation between the mediator's tasks and the required skills and attitudes.

---

18 The article *Competencies for Mediators of Complex Public Disputes*, published by the *Society of Professionals in Dispute Resolution*, provides an interesting perspective on technical expertise in the context of mediation.

TABLE 3

Correlation between tasks, skills and attitudes

TASKS	SKILLS	ATTITUDES
Frame negotiations	Manage mediation process	Leadership
Foster constructive dialogue	Manage interpersonal relations	Diplomacy
Help parties find a solution	Solve problems	Proactive

3.2.1   Framing negotiations

As manager of the mediation process, the mediator's primary task is to supervise negotiations. The framing of a negotiation may take various forms. The mediator sets and explains the ground rules and procedure for the negotiation, handles the logistics (e.g. convening meetings) and serves as intermediary between the disputing parties and outside consultants where such expertise is required. Framing negotiations is important in that the parties are rarely familiar with the mediation process and need to be guided through the various stages.

3.2.1.1   Managing the process

For negotiations to be productive, the mediator must have an acute sense of management. He or she must master the mediation process and be able to guide the parties from beginning to end. The mediator plans and supervises mediation sessions and helps discussions move toward a workable solution. As master of the negotiation process, the mediator must show strategy and vision. The ability to manage the process is all the more crucial when several parties are involved. The mediation process is described with details in chapter 4.

3.2.1.2   Leadership

Mediators must have leadership skills. They must be able to manage the mediation process while empowering the parties to determine the outcome. Leadership is of critical importance when the parties get caught up in the conflict and need guidance in their search for a solution. In order to accept the mediator's leadership, the parties must feel that he or she is trustworthy and in control of the situation. Impartiality is of the essence when allowing parties to speak, communicating information and evaluating proposals; in other words, the mediator's leadership must be non-partisan.

3.2.2   Facilitating constructive dialogue

Diametrically opposed views are a prime obstacle to constructive dialogue. In a conflict situation, the disputing parties generally have a biased view of the problem and, consequently, adopt a competitive stance. This is very human, and the mediator must temper this tendency by helping the parties take a broader look at the dispute and work cooperatively. One way to do this is to ask each party to formulate its view of the dispute.[19] Understanding how the other person sees the events that led to the problem makes it easier to appreciate his or her perspective. By encouraging the parties to imagine each other's situation, the mediator can help the parties narrow the issues and see the dispute in a different light.

Another barrier to constructive dialogue can be poor interparty communication. The main sign of this is an inability to understand the other party's concerns and proposals. When this happens, the mediator asks each party to clarify certain aspects of its proposal, measures the limits of a proposal by voicing hypotheses, and then restates the party's position, summarizing the substance of its view to make sure it is clearly understood. The mediator can also stimulate discussion by asking the parties to comment on proposals in order to identify areas of agreement and disagreement. This way, the mediator assists the parties in establishing a new level of communication conducive to constructive negotiation.

3.2.2.1 Managing interpersonal relations

Mediators must be able to create a positive atmosphere, particularly in terms of the working relationship between parties. This can be done in various ways. For instance, a sense of humour and an affable nature can go a long way towards smoothing ruffled feathers and relieving tension. Mediators must also show a certain degree of empathy, i.e. they must be sensitive to the needs and experience of each party while remaining neutral.

An ability to present options clearly is crucial as well. The way an option is presented can often mean the difference between outright rejection and a willingness to examine it more closely.[20] Remember that the mediator sets the tone for negotiations by building a working relationship between the parties. Special attention must be given to managing interpersonal relations.

---

19 The practice of "circular questioning" described by S. Cobb in *Empowerment and Mediation: A Narrative Perspective* is an interesting technique.

20 For further discussion of the presentation of proposals, see *Negotiating Rationally* by M. Bazerman and B. Neale.

3.2.2.2 Diplomacy

An essential attitude in every mediator is diplomacy. Conflict situations generally involve a certain degree of tension, which can hinder relations between the disputing parties. In fact, relations are often already broken off when the mediation process begins. The mediator needs to be receptive to the parties, listen to their needs and understand their frustrations. A sense of humour can help downplay a situation and preempt conflict escalation during the negotiation process.[21] This helps diffuse tension and fosters open dialogue. Through his or her diplomacy, the mediator encourages mutual respect between the disputing parties.

Diplomacy demands a certain degree of composure and patience. Building agreements and changing opinions take time and it is unreasonable to expect a substantial change in a party's position or attitude overnight. The mediator must respect this fact, and give the parties time to reconsider their position, no matter how long it takes. While trying to instigate change and stick to a set timeline, the mediator must manage negotiations in pace with the parties.

3.2.3 Helping parties find a solution

The mediator's third basic task is to participate more or less actively, depending on the pace of negotiations, in the problem-solving process. In an ideal situation, the parties are able to resolve the dispute on their own, in which case mediator intervention is minimal. However, most situations require that the mediator actively assist the parties in reaching an agreement. The mediator proposes alternative solutions to get the negotiation moving again. In addition, the mediator also helps the parties evaluate the costs and advantages of each option on the table.[22] Finally, he or she can help the parties better appreciate the consequences of a failed negotiation.

---

21 In *Five Elements of Mediation,* C. Honeyman describes distraction as one of the five generic types of activity engaged in by mediators.

22 For further discussion of mediator participation and party autonomy, see *Mediator Pressure and Party Autonomy: Are They Consistent with Each Other?* by D.E. Matz, and *The Proper Role of the Mediator: Rational Assessment, Not Pressure* by J.B. Boskey.

3.2.3.1   Problem-solving

Problem-solving comprises four important tasks. First, the mediator helps the parties identify the source of conflict and determine the scope of negotiations. He or she questions the parties to gain insight into the conflict and identify the underlying issues. The more aspects of the conflict that are brought to light through effective questioning, the more the proposed solutions are likely to satisfy all parties. Second, the mediator must help the parties generate proposals that will spur negotiations. One way to do this is through brainstorming. The mediator has to be able to propose a creative resolution in order to stimulate interparty negotiation. Finally, he or she aids the parties in evaluating and defining a solution.

3.2.3.2   Proactive attitude

Where necessary, the mediator must adopt a proactive stance in helping the parties find a mutually acceptable solution. In addition to overseeing the dispute resolution process, the mediator must assist the parties to devise creative alternatives. As an outsider, the mediator can suggest compromises to open the door to new solutions. It is also easier for the mediator to see options that the parties have missed.

Further, the mediator must be pragmatic. He or she must constantly verify the feasibility of each option by asking the parties to explain their proposals in detail. The disputing parties do not always have a realistic view of options, particularly when it comes to the advantages and disadvantages of those tabled by another party. So, in addition to being innovative, a mediator must be pragmatic in order to help parties determine viable solutions.

3.2.4   Expertise

Above, we examined the three principal skills required of a mediator. Obviously, this is a minimum; numerous other skills can come in handy as well. For example, the ability to communicate clearly and understand non-verbal communication such as body language is a definite asset in managing negotiations effectively. Subject matter expertise can also be useful.[23]

---

23 See *On Evaluating Mediators* by C. Honeyman.

But how much expertise does a mediator need? Consider the case of a dispute over the cleanup of a contaminated site. Would it be better if the mediator were an expert on contaminated soil? One could think that subject matter expertise is essential to successful negotiation. After all, wouldn't a mediator who knows about soil remediation automatically have a better understanding of the problem and the implications of each option?

Others consider mediator expertise secondary. Since the mediator's primary role is to help the parties negotiate their own solution, he or she must be a specialist in mediation to be able to help the disputants break a deadlock and reach an agreement. From this perspective, technical expertise may be secondary. Generally speaking, some basic knowledge of the problem is useful, but particular expertise is not indispensable. After all, the mediator can always hire an expert with the necessary technical background. The question of mediator expertise is not an easy one to answer. Clearly, however, someone who is a specialist in mediation as well as a specialist in the subject matter may have a strategic advantage.

3.3   INDIVIDUAL CHARACTERISTICS

In the previous section, we examined the mediator's tasks and attendant skills and attitudes to better describe the mediator's role. However, although all mediators perform the same role, their methods may differ. The mediator's personality will colour his or her working style. Without psychoanalysing the different types of mediator, it is worth exploring the notion of personality, particularly from the perspective of management style and bias.

3.3.1   Management style

Mediators perform the three main tasks described earlier with varying degrees of intensity depending on the case and their individual personality. Deborah Kolb identified two predominant management styles.[24] "Orchestrators" confine their actions to facilitating discussion, while "dealmakers" actively contribute to shaping an agreement. Each of these working styles has its advantages and

---

24 See *The Mediators* by D.M. Kolb.

disadvantages. Obviously, they represent extremes, and most mediators fall somewhere in the middle. In this respect, the notion of management style should not be deemed a set pattern, but rather a natural leaning, with mediators borrowing from both styles depending on the case. Table 4 compares the orchestrating and deal-making approaches to mediation.

TABLE 4

Comparison of orchestrating and dealmaking approaches to mediation

CHARACTERISTICS	DEALMAKING	ORCHESTRATING
Type of intervention	Controls negotiations	Frames negotiations
Role of mediator	Participates actively in shaping an agreement	Facilitates dialogue
Type of communication	Inducement	Clarification
Basis of concessions	Pressure from mediator	Pressure from interdependent relationship between parties

Adapted from D. Kolb, *The Mediators*, Cambridge, MIT Press, 1983.

3.3.1.1 Orchestrators

Mediators who take an orchestrating approach to dispute resolution tend to assume a passive role in negotiations. They limit their actions to framing the negotiation process, supervising discussions and encouraging parties to seek a mutually satisfactory outcome. Orchestrators give the parties substantial freedom to build their own agreement in their own time. They see their role as supporting the mediation process while empowering the parties to determine the outcome. This working style encourages parties to become partners in establishing a project or policy.

3.3.1.2 Dealmakers

In addition to framing negotiations, as an orchestrator would, dealmakers assume an active role in talks. They normally lead discussions, but may also suggest compromises. While maintaining their neutrality, they may even attempt to persuade parties to make concessions. Dealmakers see their role as "making a deal", even if it means gently twisting a few arms. The dealmaking approach is highly effective in crisis situations, where a quick solution has to be found in order to break an impasse. In such situations, the use of more heavy-handed tactics by the mediator may be appropriate.

3.3.2 Mediator bias

The notion of attitude is complex. In this book, it is restricted to the traditional model used in social psychology,[25] according to which an attitude is a mental position that can be conveyed through certain predisposed behaviour. Thus, diplomacy is a predisposition to treat parties flexibly and patiently. Along with the three basic traits described earlier, a mediator may adopt various other attitudes in dealing with certain aspects of the dispute.

A positive or negative attitude towards a particular aspect of the dispute is referred to as bias. A mediator who has a negative bias towards a project could unwittingly give citizens groups more time to speak, causing the developer to feel frustrated and withdraw from

---

25 For a more detailed explanation of the notion of attitude as used in psychology, see *Understanding Social Psychology* by S. Worchel *et al.*

the mediation process. In this sense, attitude can significantly affect the mediator's behaviour. Admitting their biases enables mediators to remain impartial.[26]

Mediators can have any number of biases, all to varying degrees. Biases fall into three general categories (Table 5). First, there are procedural biases, in which the mediator tends to employ tactics that do not necessarily reflect the dynamics of the negotiation. Second, mediators may be biased in terms of solutions. The mediator may feel that a particular settlement is more appropriate for a given type of conflict and, consequently, steer negotiations toward a resolution that may not reflect the parties' priority interests. The third type of bias has to do with partisanship; the mediator may be overly sympathetic or feel an antipathy towards one particular side. As a result, the mediator may unconsciously favour or treat a party unfairly, as the case may be, particularly when it comes to addressing their concerns or proposals.

Although the potential number of biases seems high, admitting them normally enables the mediator to control their effect on the mediation process. A mediator with a strong sense of self-awareness can remain neutral despite being biased. Remember that a bias generally translates into subjective intervention. Acknowledging their subjectivity is therefore an important step in enabling mediators to become more objective.

---

[26] For further discussion of this issue, see *Effectiveness of the Biased Mediator* by W.P. Smith.

TABLE 5

Three categories of bias

TYPE	DEFINITION
Procedure	Mediator intervenes according to his or her own inclinations instead of according to parties' needs
Solutions	Mediator steers negotiations towards the solution he or she feels is best
Partisanship	Mediator shows sympathy or dislike towards one party

3.4 SELECTING A MEDIATOR

Choosing an impartial (fair-objective-neutral) third party to oversee negotiations is an important step in the mediation process. The criteria for making this choice should include the three basic skills mentioned earlier: 1) the ability to manage the mediation process, 2) an aptitude for managing interpersonal relations and 3) a propensity for solving problems. However, the issue addressed in this section is not how to determine selection criteria, but rather how to select a mediator.[27] Can the process used to select a mediator make the situation worse or can it make the mediator's job easier? This section examines two means of selecting a mediator: by designation or by consensus.

3.4.1 Designation

The first method for choosing a mediator is to designate one. This is usually done by an individual or public body with no vested interests. A minister or municipality, for example, can designate a mediator to act as non-partisan intermediary between a project promoter and citizens groups. While designation is an efficient way to choose a mediator, it can raise doubts as to impartiality. Stakeholding parties that are not involved in the selection process may question the neutrality of a politically appointed mediator.

Having the mediator designated by a public body that is far-removed from the conflict helps reduce this perception. The president, chairman or director of the organization appoints someone from its bank of mediators after ascertaining that there is no conflict of interest. This avoids additional conflict between the parties over the choice of mediator, while ensuring impartiality, since the mediator is chosen by an uninvolved public body.[28]

---

27 On selecting a mediator, see *Quality Dispute Resolution: How Can You Be Assured of Quality Service?* by P. Field.

28 Designation is used by Quebec's environmental hearings board (BAPE) to select mediators in disputes requiring mediation. See *Environmental Officials in Quebec Serve as Mediators* by P. Renaud.

3.4.2 Consensus

Mediators can also be chosen by consensus. Rather than being designated, the mediator is selected by the disputing parties. They can consult a private conflict management service, which will provide a list of certified mediators or persons with natural mediation skills. Or, the selection process can be overseen by a government body. In this case, the parties are given a list of names from which they choose the mediator that best suits their needs and who inspires the most confidence. Consensual selection has certain advantages. First, the parties feel they are getting an impartial mediator whose expertise is in keeping with their mutual needs. On the other hand, they may have trouble agreeing on a mediator, thereby creating a new disagreement that only compounds the original dispute and leads to unwanted delays.

Theoretical distinctions aside, it would be incorrect to conclude that selecting a mediator from a list of specialists is necessarily the best option. The essential element in making a judicious choice, no matter how that choice is made, is that all parties have confidence in the mediator's neutrality and competence. Whether the mediator is chosen by one of the disputing parties or by a public body, if these two principles are respected, the choice is a good one. While some selection processes are more likely to inspire party confidence, it is the degree of perceived confidence and competency that are important and not the means by which they are obtained.

3.5 SUMMARY

In our analysis of the mediator's role, we have attempted to establish a connection between the mediator's tasks and the skills and attitudes required to carry them out. The mediator's role can be summarized in terms of three basic activities: the mediator ensures that negotiations are carried out in a setting conducive to dispute resolution, helps the parties explore various options in order to determine a mutually acceptable solution, and fosters a constructive working relationship between the parties, particularly as concerns the presentation and mutual understanding of viewpoints. Depending on the mandate, the mediator can adopt either an "orchestrating" or a "deal-making" role. Finally, mediators can be designated by an outside body or they can be selected by the disputing parties. The tasks performed by a mediator can be separated into two categories. So-called general tasks, which are predicated on the mediation process and apply to all mediation, include establishing the framework for and supervising negotiations. Specific tasks depend on the dynamics of the negotiation and are determined on a case-by-case basis. Examples include helping the parties resolve their dispute and facilitating constructive dialogue. The next chapter expands on the mediator's general tasks, i.e. mediation as such, while Chapter 5 looks at the specific tasks, or the dynamics of negotiation.

Chapter 4

The Mediation Process

CHAPTER 4

THE MEDIATION PROCESS

4.1 EFFICIENT FRAMING

As discussed in the previous chapter, the general task required of all mediators entails framing negotiations. Efficient framing encourages problem-solving and promotes constructive dialogue. The different stages of the mediation process presented in this chapter focus on problem-solving while allowing negotiations to unfold naturally.[29] Consequently, mediation can be seen as an extension of negotiations. A structured process informs the mediator on the strategies and tactics to employ, and facilitates orderly intervention.

Regardless of the type of dispute, the resolution process is substantially the same. Without trying to equate mediation with cooking, the following analogy seems apt. If you take a close look at the recipes, all omelettes, whether Spanish, western or ham and cheese, are made in much the same way. Only the ingredients change. The same holds true for mediation and the reconciliation of interests in public disputes. The mediation process consists of a number of successive stages and steps that provide the framework for negotiations and effective dispute resolution.

It is important to note that the mediation process has been systematized into four main phases based on the theory of

---

29 For further reading on the negotiation process, see *Negotiation Theory and Practice* by J.W. Breslin and J.Z. Rubin.

problem-solving.[30] The planning phase serves to define the problem. The source of the problem is identified in the analysis phase, followed by the negotiation of a solution during the mediation phase. The final phase consists in implementing the solution. The four phases are carried out in succession and each one must be completed before the next one is possible (Table 6).

The process described in this chapter is extremely flexible and is intended as an outline of the activities involved in mediated negotiation.[31] It is easily adaptable to widely different management styles, disputes and institutions that offer, or plan to offer, public mediation services.

---

[30] For additional reading on problem-solving, see *Résoudre un problème : méthode et outils pour une meilleure qualité* by A.-M. Chauvel.

[31] The process presented in this chapter is inspired in part by the mediation process developed by Quebec's environmental hearings board (BAPE) and described in *La médiation en environnement au BAPE : un processus administratif et public* and *The Environmental Assessment Process and Public Participation in Québec: Concrete Elements for Sustainable Development* by P. Renaud. Also see *New Approaches to Resolving Local Public Disputes* by D. Madigan *et al.*, *Breaking the Impasse: Consensual Approaches to Resolving Public Disputes* by L. Susskind and J. Cruikshank, and *Environmental Mediation As an Alternative to Litigation: The Emerging Practice and Limitations* by J.W. Blackburn.

TABLE 6

Phases of the mediation process

PLANNING	ANALYSIS	MEDIATION	IMPLEMENTATION
– Identifying parties	– Fact-finding	– Generating options	– Signing the agreement
– Assessing the conflict	– Identifying points in contention	– Assessing options	– Monitoring implementation and modifying the agreement
– Handling logistics	– Identifying sources of escalation	– Determining a solution	– Checking compliance
– Explaining the process	– Setting a negotiation agenda	– Preparing a draft agreement	
– Organizing parties		– Improving the agreement	

4.2   THE PLANNING PHASE

The planning phase is aimed at laying the groundwork for negotiations. The fact that the parties agree to a consensual approach
does not, in itself, mean they are ready to start negotiating: getting
parties to commit to mediation takes time. The mediator must also
make sure that the prerequisites for successful mediation (see
Chapter 2) exist before beginning the process. Since poorly prepared
negotiations are not likely to result in a mutually beneficial agreement, the planning stage precedes negotiations and includes five
specific steps: identifying the parties, assessing the conflict, handling
logistics, explaining the mediation process, and organizing the parties.

4.2.1   Identifying the parties

Identifying the stakeholding parties consists in determining who
should sit at the negotiating table and whether they agree to do so.
It is important that as many of the parties as possible, if not all,
cooperate in this step in order to avoid further conflict later on, should
someone be unhappy with the negotiated settlement. A lasting solution hinges on the involvement of all parties.

Identifying parties can be relatively easy when their names appear
in legal proceedings, if they have filed a claim with the government
or if they are a municipality. It is harder when the parties are not
clearly associated with the dispute, such as an interest group that
has not yet taken formal steps because it is waiting for the outcome
or final project, or groups that may only be affected in the future. It
is therefore important that the mediator identify not only the immediate parties to the dispute, but anyone who may become involved
later on.

4.2.2   Assessing the conflict

Step 2 of the planning phase has several components. The first
question that needs to be asked is "Is the dispute likely to be resolved
through mediation?". As seen in Chapter 2, mediation is not a definitive conflict management method. The issues involved in the project
or policy must be identified before opting for this technique. The prerequisites for successful mediation (Chapter 2, Table 2) are an

excellent reference for evaluating the potential for resolution. When all four prerequisites are present, there is every chance for settlement. The parties' awareness of the consequences of a failed negotiation and of the mutual gain possible through agreement also helps determine whether the conflict is "ripe" for settlement.[32] When assessing the conflict, the mediator must never lose sight of its perception by the parties, which is just as important as the actual conflict.

4.2.3   Handling logistics

Handling logistics is an unavoidable step in planning negotiations. Things as simple as scheduling and deciding where to hold mediation sessions, accommodating parties (e.g. conference room, transportation) and following up on information (e.g. letter writing) can become extremely complicated the more participants there are. Careful planning of logistics is vital to establishing an appropriate, efficient framework for negotiations, which is why more than half the time spent on a single mediation mandate can go to coordinating meetings.

4.2.4   Explaining the process

Explaining the mediation process to the parties involves introducing the mediator and explaining his or her training, experience and present mandate. The parties are also informed of the various stages in the process and all applicable legislation. By the end of this step, the parties should know what to expect and should understand the mediator's role as a non-partisan facilitator.

The mediator can also use this step to make technical decisions. For instance, the parties can agree on certain ground rules, such as no public statements during the negotiation. If desired, the mediator can also impose his or her own ground rules. In addition, the parties and mediator can set a deadline for reaching an agreement, and decide what steps will be taken should negotiations fail. Clear game rules avoid additional conflict during the negotiation process, and let the parties know what to expect and what is required of them.

---

32 See *Some Wise and Mistaken Assumptions About Conflict and Negotiation* by J.Z. Rubin.

4.2.5   Organizing parties

Another crucial step in the planning stage is organizing parties in preparation for negotiations. Certain groups or parties may not be sufficiently organized to participate effectively in the process. For example, a party may not have an official spokesperson, or, even if the group is unanimously for or against the project or policy, the group's negotiating representatives may not have clear objectives. The parties may also have very little experience in negotiation. For all of these reasons, it is important that the mediator help structure the disputing parties so they are ready to negotiate.[33]

For instance, the mediated negotiation of a project to build a small craft harbour in Sandspit, British Columbia, was apparently rendered more difficult, despite a successful outcome, by a lack of organization among the promoter's representatives. Some participants criticized the fact that the promoter had not been clearly identified.[34]

The mediator can also help party representatives define a mandate that sets out clear objectives for negotiation. To ensure that commitments will be upheld, it is crucial that the group's spokesperson have the support of the majority of members. Negotiation objectives can be defined by polling members, voting, or holding consultations. In some cases, the mediator and the disputing parties may deem it useful to form subcommittees comprised of a representative from each party.

In some cases, it may also be useful to provide participants with pre-negotiation training to ensure that discussions are as productive as possible. If parties are not experienced in negotiation or are accustomed to resolving disputes based on an adversarial model, discussions can deteriorate into endless arguing, instead of focusing on joint problem-solving. Training parties in negotiation can result in better interparty communication during mediation.

4.3   THE ANALYSIS PHASE

Phase 2 of the mediation process is analysis. The mediator works with the parties to identify the nature and source of the conflict in

---

33 For more on party organization, see *Negotiation Basics: Concept, Skills and Exercises* by R.A. Johnson.
34 See *Sandspit Small Craft Harbour Mediation Process* by the Canadian Environmental Assessment Agency.

order to determine the issues that need to be negotiated to resolve it. The primary causes of conflict include opposing goals or means and the various sources of escalation underlying it. During the analysis phase, the mediator must determine the facts, define the points of contention and identify the substantive issues. The information gathered during these steps is used to set a negotiation agenda.

4.3.1   Fact-finding

The first step in the analysis phase consists of establishing the facts. The mediator must separate fact from fiction, determine what is real and what is interpretation, conviction or probability.[35] A noisy environment is a personal appreciation; a noise level of 90 decibels is a fact. Collecting all relevant background information is important for diagnosing the conflict, as it will subsequently serve as a basis for negotiations. To this end, the mediator can recommend additional studies and analyses in order to round out the information gathered. At the same time, the mediator can query parties on their perception of the facts; he or she must accept those perceptions for what they are.

The information gathered and exchanged during the analysis phase may even be sufficient for resolving part of the dispute. For example, during the mediated negotiation of a project to build a new electrical substation in Candiac, Québec, discussions between a citizen and project promoters regarding the effects of the electromagnetic fields of power lines were enough to partially resolve the conflict. In fact, the mediation setting had enabled such constructive dialogue that, by the end of the discussions, the citizen no longer opposed the project.[36]

4.3.2   Identifying points of contention

The mediator uses fact-finding to identify the points of contention in the project. This step is aimed at gaining insight into the areas of disagreement, and helping the parties understand each other's posi-

---

35 See *Six chapeaux pour penser* by E. De Bono.
36 See *Construction du poste de distribution Roussillon à 315 kV-25 kV et d'une ligne de dérivation biterne à 315 kV à Laprairie* by the Bureau d'audiences publiques sur l'environnement.

tion. The disputants are often too caught up in their own view of the conflict to be able to see the other side. Identifying the points of contention provides an excellent opportunity to explore mutual interests and needs. Through proper questioning, the mediator can help the parties define the scope of their interests and their differing goals. Does the party really want to see the plant shut down and hundreds of jobs lost, or does it just want to make sure the plant reduces its toxic emissions to a minimum?

During this step, it is important that discussions focus on mutual understanding and acceptance of interests, and not on positions. The points of contention can generally be grouped into substantive issues. For example, the combined noise level, visual pollution and loss of privacy resulting from road construction can threaten certain residents' quality of life. Grouping elements of disagreement into substantive issues not only provides a comprehensive view of the problem, but also highlights the needs and values involved in the dispute. Furthermore, analyzing party priorities and the differences therein enables an integrative view of the relationship between conflicting positions.[37]

4.3.3   Identifying sources of escalation

Another important dimension of analysis is identifying sources of escalation. Have legal proceedings been instituted? Have any of the parties made a public statement that is apt to lock them into their position? Is there a history of conflict between any of the parties? These and other sources of escalation will affect the negotiation process. For example, if some of the parties have been in dispute before, they may come to the negotiating table with tremendous apprehension. Identifying sources of escalation is critical, as it enables the mediator to develop strategies for reducing them in order to create a positive dynamic for negotiation. These aspects will be discussed in the next chapter, in conjunction with the management of interpersonal relations during mediation.

---

[37] For further reading on this issue, see *Common Elements in the Analysis of the Negotiation Process* by I.W. Zartman.

4.3.4 Setting a negotiation agenda

The final step in the analysis phase consists in setting an agenda. Since the information gathered throughout this phase paves the way for mediated negotiation, a negotiation agenda can be a very useful tool. Basically, it consists in grouping the points of contention and substantive issues into topics of negotiation. To set the agenda, the mediator focuses on the issues that need to be resolved for a settlement to be reached. Knowing the possible sources of escalation can be useful for the strategic organization of negotiation topics. For instance, certain matters will be better addressed at the end, while others will be useful for getting discussions under way. An agenda that defines common objectives for negotiation makes it easier to forge a settlement.[38]

4.4 THE MEDIATION PHASE

Phase 3 of the dispute resolution process is mediated negotiation. The planning and analysis phases lay the groundwork for and identify the bases of negotiation, while the actual mediation process serves to build a consensus on a workable option for the project or policy in dispute. Since it is highly unlikely that the parties will agree to the first option put forward, mediation involves gradually shaping options into a consensual solution. This phase involves five main steps: generating options, assessing options, determining a solution, preparing a draft agreement and improving the agreement.

4.4.1 Generating options

With the mediator's assistance, the parties identify their concerns, needs and priorities during the analysis phase. These will serve as the parameters for formulating options during Step 1 of the mediation phase. All options that integrate the disputants' individual needs and priorities are potential acceptable solutions. Before they can determine the best solution, however, the parties must generate as many options as possible and formulate them into a proposal that is supported by all sides. Brainstorming can be particularly useful for

---

38 See *We Need a Larger Theory of Negotiation: The Importance of Pre-Negotiating Phases* by H.H. Saunders.

finding as many extemporaneous options as possible.[39] During brainstorming sessions, the parties spontaneously suggest proposals that are consistent with the parameters established during the exploration of interests.

At this point, it is important that rationalization not hinder the parties' imagination. Two simple rules will ensure that brainstorming is successful. First, the mediator must inform the parties that their ideas will not be assessed immediately. Second, it must be noted that these are ideas and in no way constitute a commitment; the parties will not be bound by any of the options proposed. The mediator should create a dynamic that encourages maximum creativity.

Brainstorming serves two purposes: it allows the parties to discover creative solutions and shows them that there is more than one way to solve a problem. During the mediated negotiation of a project to turn a two-lane highway near Bromptonville, Québec, into a four-lane highway, the disputants realized that the only way to reduce the noise level to the OECD standard of 55 dD(A) was to move a resident's house farther back on his lot. This case exemplifies the innovative character of mediation in that the parties eventually realized that an initially outrageous proposal was, in fact, the only viable solution.[40]

4.4.2　Assessing options

After generating as many options as possible, the parties and the mediator need to assess them. Those that are deemed unfeasible, either because they are too costly or too difficult to implement, are discarded. The remaining options can then be evaluated, a difficult task at best. The high number of interests at stake, parties involved and possible trades can result in packages that are so complex that assessment is impossible without an orderly procedure. A single negotiating text can be an efficient way to systematize this task.

The "single-text" negotiation procedure, described by Roger Fisher,[41] is a strategy whereby the mediator develops a single nego-

---

39 On the process of brainstorming, see *Résoudre un problème : méthode et outils pour une meilleure qualité* by A.-M. Chauvel.

40 See *Autoroute 55 : doublement de la chaussée entre Bromptonville et l'intersection avec le chemin de la Rivière* by the Bureau d'audiences publiques sur l'environnement.

41 See *Playing the Wrong Game?* by R. Fisher.

tiating text around the option he or she feels is the most popular and then submits the final draft to the parties for comment. Any changes must be negotiated between the disputants. The mediator rewrites the text, incorporating the changes, and then submits it to the parties for feedback and renegotiation. The procedure is repeated until the parties reach a final agreement. Elements from other options can be integrated at any time during the negotiation process.

4.4.3   Determining a solution

When assessing options, the parties must regularly make choices. Whether these choices involve deciding on a single provision or an entire settlement, the way in which they are made affects the quality of the final agreement. Two main approaches can be taken. First, the parties can argue their respective cases to determine who is right or who wins. While this may be a natural reaction, it is not the best approach, since it may inflame the debate and nullify any progress towards a settlement. As a rule, no one is willing to cede. And even if someone does end up ceding and there is a winner, it does not necessarily mean that the best solution prevailed.

Parties can also make choices based on objective criteria, the second approach to decision-making.[42] They begin by agreeing on one or more criteria and then decide which option best meets the chosen criteria. These can be a government standard, the findings of a scientific study, a recommendation from a specialist or past experience with a similar case.

4.4.4   Preparing a draft agreement

Once the parameters of a mutually acceptable solution have been defined and accepted, a detailed written agreement is drafted. In some cases, the mediator can use the negotiating text as a basis. However, in cases where the mediator wants or needs to draft a new agreement from scratch, he or she can either do it alone or with the parties' help. If the mediator chooses to draft the agreement alone, he or she can simply refine the negotiating text into a final

---

42 A technique of principled negotiation described by R. Fisher and W.L. Ury in *Getting to YES: Negotiating Agreement Without Giving In.*

agreement and ask the parties to ratify it. While this is by far the easiest way to proceed, there is always a chance that the final agreement will not be exactly what the parties expected. Drafting it together avoids such surprises and allows changes and adjustments to be made along the way.

4.4.5   Improving the agreement

Despite the parties' efforts to formulate the best possible option, they may very well have missed some mutual gains. They may be too close to the situation to see the whole picture. Or, they may come up with new and interesting ideas after an agreement has already been reached. Adding a step that enables the parties to enhance the agreement can therefore be both appropriate and of strategic value.

The post-settlement settlement strategy, proposed by Howard Raiffa,[43] consists in the mediator's suggesting ways to improve the written agreement. The proposed changes are designed to capitalize on elements that have been overlooked by the parties in order to achieve a mutual-gain outcome without causing prejudice to any one side. Where warranted, this task can also be entrusted to an outside expert. The revised agreement is submitted to the parties, who are entitled to veto the new proposal. Should it be rejected by even one party, the original agreement stands.

This strategy has its advantages, but also its risks. The enhanced agreement can cause a consensus to fall through, and require certain aspects of the agreement to be renegotiated. It may be preferable to adopt a more conservative approach and stick with the original agreement. However, this will largely depend on the parties' working relationship and the mediator's skill in suggesting win-win solutions. Moreover, it is the mediator who decides whether improving the agreement is appropriate for the case at hand.

---

43 See *Post-Settlement Settlements* by H. Raiffa.

4.5 THE IMPLEMENTATION PHASE

Implementation, the fourth and final phase of mediation, is aimed at transforming the negotiated settlement into a lasting solution. Several steps are involved in achieving this objective. First, the agreement developed by the parties must be made official. Second, the parties must design mechanisms for ensuring that the project is executed or the policy administered according to the terms of the agreement. Such mechanisms can include a monitoring committee or instruments for modifying the agreement. Third, a final meeting may be deemed necessary to verify that the conditions of the agreement have been respected to the satisfaction of all parties. Once these three steps are complete, the mediation process is officially over.

4.5.1 Signing the agreement

The final agreement must be signed by each of the parties to make it official. Although this may seem like a fast, easy step, it can actually be complicated. Some parties may have to take the agreement back to their constituants for a vote before signing. In this case, the mediator must make sure the parties do not use the occasion to wrest last-minute concessions. Others may make their ratification contingent on certain conditions. For example, a party may recognize the agreement as binding only if the budget provided for is respected. Should it double, the party reserves the right to withdraw its ratification. Finally, a party may demand that another party commit to the agreement before it agrees to sign. These are just a few of the problems a mediator might face in getting the final signatures.

4.5.2 Monitoring implementation and modifying the agreement

A negotiated settlement does not necessarily mean a definitive agreement. Certain aspects of the agreement and the specific nature of the project or policy may require follow-up. For example, an agreement may stipulate maximum pollution levels, in which case the latter will have to be measured at prescribed intervals. A group or committee to monitor implementation may have to be created.

Furthermore, establishing procedures for managing future conflicts arising from the agreement's implementation can be crucial to sustaining consensus. New issues may surface or the terms of the agreement may require amending as a result of new information. A monitoring committee may be composed of constituents from each party or be formed by a mutually agreed upon independent body.

The purpose of a monitoring committee is to ensure full compliance with the negotiated settlement. Although such a committee is not always necessary, a party may make it a condition for signing the agreement. When such a committee is formed, the parties determine what is to be measured, how measurements are to be taken, and what powers the committee is to hold. For example, opponents and promoters of a project to dredge a private harbour in Baie-Comeau, Québec, used mediation to develop a joint protocol for monitoring water quality during operations.[44]

4.5.3   Checking compliance

The last step in the implementation phase consists in consulting the parties to see that the conditions of the agreement have been complied with in full. This basically means confirming that the dispute has been resolved and that the file can be closed. This potentially easy step involves going through the agreement provision by provision to check for compliance. The process is a little more complicated when the objective is achieved over time, such as a maximum pollution level, in which case, a more in-depth analysis and follow-up may be needed to determine whether objectives have been attained. This last step is also of symbolic value, as it serves to strengthen the partnership ties developed during negotiations.

4.6   USEFULNESS OF A PROCEDURAL APPROACH

Certain aspects of the mediation model presented in this chapter may seem categorical and therefore raise questions. Need it be followed to the letter? Is it possible to skip certain steps? First, it is important to remember that the purpose of mediation is not to impose

---

44 See *Programme décennal de dragage aux abords des quais de Cargill Limitée à Baie-Comeau* by the Bureau d'audiences publiques sur l'environnement.

a specific procedure, but rather to guide the mediator and parties through a series of steps that gradually lead to consensus. These steps follow a logical and chronological progression requiring that one stage be completed before the next begins. For example, it would be counterproductive to begin negotiating before identifying the concerns and interests of each party. Unfortunately, this is often what happens and parties end up negotiating without even understanding the other side's position. Parties then negotiate without having a common understanding of what represents an element of discussion for the other.

A step-by-step procedure helps avoid this type of mistake. Moreover, certain factors associated with the procedural aspect of mediation can either facilitate or hinder the process, depending on whether they are positive or negative. Being aware of these factors is important, since they are common to all mediation efforts (Figure 6).

FIGURE 6

Factors affecting the mediation process

NEGATIVE FACTORS

Confusion over roles

Poorly framed
negotiations

Negotiations that move
too fast or too slowly

POSITIVE FACTORS

Party commitment to
negotiate in good faith

Creation of subcommittees
to discuss options

Responsible attitude on
the part of parties

4.6.1 Factors with a negative impact

Since every dispute is unique, the problems associated with nego-tiation are as diverse as they are numerous. However, by limiting ourselves to the procedural aspects of mediation as described in this chapter, we can identify three common problems: lack of clear roles (parties and mediator); poor negotiation framing; and negotiations that move too fast or too slowly. These factors can adversely affect the mediation process because they stall negotiations. The mediator can avoid or overcome them by developing case-specific strategies and tactics.

4.6.1.1 Confusion over roles

One of the problems that can arise during mediation is that con-fusion arises over the parties' respective roles.[45] It is important to remember that the disputants' perception of their role dictates their actions. Roles may be unclear because they overlap, i.e. a party may hinder the mediator's intervention by assuming a co-mediator role in attempting to steer discussions, impose a schedule or stipu-late a specific negotiation procedure. It is important that the mediator clearly define the role of each player, particularly in terms of authority over the mediation process. Roles may also become confused when a subgroup or committee does not have an official spokesperson, i.e. no team leader to enunciate the group's needs. In this case, the mediator needs to help the parties get organized for effective action by appointing someone to speak for them. Clearly defined roles provide structure for negotiations and allow for more productive exchanges.

4.6.1.2 Poorly framed negotiations

Negotiations that are poorly framed can be as problematic as con-fusion over roles. If the issues to be negotiated are not clearly defined or properly organized during the analysis phase, discussions during the mediation phase may be unfocused and slow-going. Poor framing can lead parties to negotiate several aspects of a problem simulta-neously, when they should be dealt with separately.[46] For example, it may be important to negotiate a regulation regarding a sewer

---

45 See *Multilateral Negotiation: An Analytic Approach* by S. Touval.
46 See *Interests: The Measure of Negotiation* by D.A. Lax and J.K. Sebenius.

system by considering the various regions serviced by the system individually, since different regions may have different characteristics, needs and interests. During the negotiation of a project to clean up the waters of Fisher Point, in the city of Lac-Brôme, Québec, the parties became deadlocked primarily because no environmental distinction had been made between Fisher Point East and Fisher Point West.[47] Poor framing can also cause discussions to stray from the negotiable aspects of a project, leading parties to debate issues that are unrelated to the problem, thereby precluding resolution. A well-prepared mediation plan is indispensable to the efficient framing of items for negotiation.

4.6.1.3 Negotiations that move too fast or too slowly

The pace of negotiations is another important factor. A typical mistake is to insist on speed. When this happens, the mediator and parties start discussing proposed solutions before exploring individual interests and concerns. While it is possible for parties to reach a settlement without exploring their mutual interests, it is not possible for them to shape a solution that maximizes mutual gain without exploring and understanding each others' needs. In their haste to formulate an agreement, the parties may overlook worthwhile options. While encouraging the parties to find a solution, it is important that the mediator make sure they do not skip any steps in the mediation process, no matter how superfluous they may seem.

Another problem with negotiating too fast is failure to respect the process of change. Changing attitudes and perceptions takes time, particularly for parties that have been locked in conflict for a long period. In expediting negotiations, the mediator may only make parties more reluctant to rethink their position. When given time to reflect, those same parties may eventually come to support another option. In managing the negotiation process, the mediator should be mindful of and respect the pace of each party, even if it means moving more slowly.

On the other hand, negotiations that move too slowly can be just as problematic. Some progress is needed to keep parties motivated. If negotiation is too slow, certain parties may get discouraged and

---

47 See *Projet d'assainissement des eaux Pointe Fisher Ouest, Ville de Lac Brome* by the Bureau d'audiences publiques sur l'environnement.

walk away from the table. Slow-moving negotiations can also cause parties to threaten the other side into making concessions or stop negotiating altogether and find another way to achieve their goal. The pace of negotiations can intensify the conflict and prevent parties from finding a resolution. The mediator must be careful to ensure that negotiations unfold at just the right speed.

4.6.2 Factors with a positive impact

Just as negative factors can hinder negotiations, positive factors can facilitate consensus-building. Positive factors include a commitment to negotiate in good faith, the creation of subcommittees and a responsible attitude on the part of the parties. While other factors are just as crucial to successful mediation, these three warrant further discussion as they are common to every mediation effort.

4.6.2.1 Commitment to negotiate in good faith

The parties' willingness to negotiate a solution is critical to the mediation process. Some parties may come to the negotiating table uncommitted, and continually threaten to leave at the slightest stumbling block. Although mediation is a voluntary process, it is important that the parties commit to making an active contribution to finding the best possible solution. At any time during the process, the parties are free to reject a solution they deem unsatisfactory. Committing to settle in good faith helps foster a positive attitude and encourage parties to play a more active role in the negotiation process. The impact of such a psychological commitment on the process should not be overlooked.

4.6.2.2 Creation of subgroups to discuss options

The multilateral or multidimensional nature of negotiations in public disputes can make logistics more complicated. When several players are involved, it may be impossible to consider each group's individual interests and proposals. If there are ten groups and each group studies every other group's options, the number of opinions increases exponentially and managing the negotiation becomes arduous. Forming subgroups can be extremely useful, even indispensable, for sound management.[48] It greatly decreases the number of options on the negotiating table, since the parties can submit a shared proposal. A subgroup is generally composed of parties that share common concerns or needs. It is of utmost importance that each subgroup be given a clear, specific mandate; for example, formulating the guiding principles for a negotiation topic.

4.6.2.3 *Responsible attitude on the part of parties*

Attitudes are critical for the mediation process, since the parties' approach to the conflict sets the tone for negotiations. Mediation has been shown to be more productive when the promoter assumes responsibility for a project.[49] A responsible attitude involves willingness to compensate for a project's disadvantages, and damages in the event of unforeseen impacts. A responsible attitude does not necessarily mean that the promoter promises to meet all demands unconditionally, but rather that it is ready to back up the provisions of the agreement with some kind of guarantee. For example, the promoter can suggest enhancing a marsh to offset the loss of an ecosystem, or carrying out the necessary remedial measures should the noise level of a construction site exceed the regulated standards.

A positive attitude on the part of project opponents is just as important. In this respect, flexible negotiation objectives can provide some much-appreciated leeway. When parties express their opposition through minimum objectives to be met before allowing a project to go ahead, negotiation is easier than when that opposition is expressed in the form of hard-and-fast options. For example, it is easier to negotiate how an environmental standard is to be met than it is the construction *sine qua non* of a multimillion-dollar treatment plant. A positive attitude is closely tied to the parties' willingness to explore areas of disagreement and seek a win-win outcome. It is of utmost importance that the mediator foster a positive attitude during the planning phase.

---

48 For further reading on subgroups in the context of negotiations, see *Multilateral Negotiation: An Analytic Approach* by S. Touval.
49 See *Moving Communities from "NIMBY" to "YIMBY"* by H. Kunreuther.

4.7   SUMMARY

In this chapter, we have examined the mediation process in terms of how the mediator plans negotiations, diagnoses the conflict, supervises discussions and ensures implementation of the negotiated agreement. Another use of an organized mediation process comes from the fact that all conflicts follow the same step in their resolution. An orderly procedure such as this provides structure and is applicable to all types of public or private-sector disputes. The parties' commitment to negotiate in good faith, the creation of subgroups to discuss options, and a responsible attitude can facilitate management of the mediation process.

Disputes are also affected by the human factor. Relations between parties can be marked by anger or frustration, and the nature of the conflict can lead parties to adopt an attitude that inflames discussions. Parties may also react to a given situation due to a lack of information or knowledge. These psychological aspects are referred to as the dynamics of the negotiation process. Unlike the mediation procedure, the strategies and tactics employed by the mediator in response to conflict dynamics are case-specific, depending on the situation or the group in question. Together, these aspects of the mediator's actions form the "art of mediation", which is the subject of the next chapter.

Chapter 5

The Dynamics of
the Negotiation Process

CHAPTER 5

THE DYNAMICS OF THE NEGOTIATION PROCESS

5.1 A POSITIVE CLIMATE CONDUCIVE TO CONSTRUCTIVE DIALOGUE

The previous chapter detailed how the mediation procedure can be used to frame and structure negotiations. However, mediation is not simply a mechanical sequence of steps; it is also a dynamic process. The type of situation, the participants' personalities, the specifics of the conflict and the mediator-party relationship are all important variables in the mediation process. These variables, which vary greatly from one dispute to the next and transcend the procedural framework of mediation, constitute the dynamics of the negotiation process.

Whereas the framework of mediated negotiation can be seen linearly (i.e. a logical sequence of steps), the dynamics of the process must be seen globally. These dynamics are substantially influenced by the quality of the disputants' interpersonal relations and how productively they work to resolve their differences. For the same process, the tone can vary from one mediation to the next: it can be tense and competitive, or productive and cooperative. The dynamics determine the atmosphere in which mediation takes place; creating an atmosphere conducive to conflict resolution is just as important as managing the process itself. Even the best process will not lead to a consensual agreement if the mediator is unable to create a positive climate in which constructive negotiation is possible.

The mediator must constantly intervene to foster and create a positive dynamic. This can be achieved by focusing on two dimensions of mediation: interpersonal relations and productive problem-solving. Table 7 shows the dimensions and components of negotiation dynamics in relation to the specific tasks performed by the mediator (Figure 5, Chapter 3). This chapter explores how mediators can build on these aspects to help create a positive dynamic for negotiation.

TABLE 7

Principal components of negotiation dynamics

DIMENSION	SPECIFIC TASKS OF MEDIATOR	PRINCIPAL COMPONENTS
Interpersonal relations	Foster constructive dialogue	Trust
		Cooperation
Productive problem-solving	Help parties find a solution	Active behaviour
		Consensus

5.2 INTERPERSONAL RELATIONS IN THE MEDIATION CONTEXT

Human relations are an important factor in the dynamics of the negotiation process. After all, the disputants are first and foremost human beings. The very existence of conflict can cause them to be mistrusting and adopt a competitive stance, creating an obstacle to constructive exchanges. And if the parties do not trust one another, it may be impossible for the mediator to deflate the conflict. How can parties be convinced to postpone legal proceedings if they are highly suspicious of each other? Each party will be afraid of being taken advantage of by the other. A minimum of cooperation is therefore needed to reconcile the parties' diverging interests. Indeed, eliciting concessions can be hard when the atmosphere is competitive. The mediator must help the parties establish a trusting relationship and work cooperatively in order to create a positive atmosphere for negotiation.

5.2.1 Establishing a trusting relationship

It is important that the mediator-party relationship be built on trust; otherwise, the parties will be far more likely to engage in defensive communication, refuse proposals and be reluctant to communicate their interests. Creating a climate of mutual trust is therefore vital to productive negotiation. But while there is little the mediator can do about the degree of trust between the parties, he or she can do something to gain the parties' trust in the mediator and in the process.[50] This confidence subsequently shapes the parties' own interaction. Five strategies are particularly useful in this regard: explaining the process, consulting the parties, employing a progressive approach, maintaining impartiality, and fostering active listening. Figure 7 shows how these strategies combine to create a trusting relationship.

5.2.1.1 Explaining the process

Parties generally come to the negotiating table with very little experience in mediation. If they harbour doubts about the process, they

---

[50] On establishing trust in the context of mediation, see *La médiation : le rôle et la dynamique de la confiance entre les parties* by J. Poitras.

may become defensive. In explaining the process to them, the mediator must help the parties feel secure. He or she should carefully explain each step, specifying the role of each player. This way, the parties know what to expect and can focus on the substance of discussions. If deemed appropriate, the mediator should feel free to go over the procedure a second time to make sure there is no confusion. Since the majority of parties attending mediation sessions usually do not know what the process is all about, they may be mistrusting and extremely hesitant to take part in negotiations. They may fear that their participation will be taken as a sign that they either approve the project or are in a weak negotiating position. Given that the reconciliation of interests through face-to-face discussion is a relatively new concept in the mediation of public disputes, explaining the process is crucial in winning the confidence of the parties.

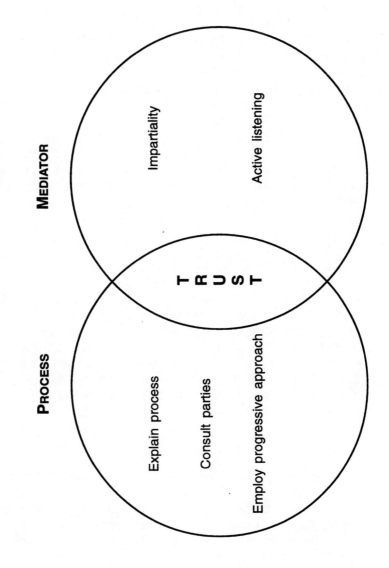

FIGURE 7

Building a trusting relationship

MEDIATOR

Impartiality

Active listening

PROCESS

Explain process

Consult parties

Employ progressive approach

T
R
U
S
T

5.2.1.2 Consulting the parties

Although the mediator is in charge of the mediation process, he or she should consult the parties before making a decision. This does not mean that the parties decide on procedure; it means that the mediator asks their advice before making a final decision. For example, if discussions get too stormy, the mediator might ask the parties if they wish to adjourn or continue the session another day. Even if the mediator knows full well that this move is vital to the process, just asking the party's permission involves them in the procedure and respects the voluntary nature of mediation. The mediator sends the indirect message that he or she will not act without the parties' consent. Should a party refuse to give its consent, the mediator can explain why he or she thinks this decision is crucial to moving negotiations forward. The more the parties feel a part of procedural decisions, the more likely they are to accept the process and trust the mediator.[51]

5.2.1.3 Employing a progressive approach

The negotiation process is above all a process of change. The parties gradually modify their position to arrive at a mutually satisfactory solution. This change implies progression, and progression implies pace. A mediator who wants to gain parties' trust must respect their pace of change. If you were helping someone with a broken leg get down the stairs, you would proceed one step at a time; if you tried to take two steps at a time, the person might get frightened, if not fall. The same is true for mediation. A step-by-step approach that respects the pace of the parties is crucial to building a trusting relationship.

5.2.1.4 Maintaining impartiality

When giving his or her views of a proposal, the mediator must consider all sides. Listing all possible options, even the obvious ones, reinforces the mediator's neutrality and prevents any one party from feeling injured or controlled. By presenting his or her ideas neutrally, the mediator maintains the role of impartial intermediary. The mediator must also make sure the process is fair.[52] This is accomplished

---

51 The principle of consulting before deciding is developed in *Getting Together: Building Relationships as We Negotiate* by R. Fisher and S. Brown.

52 See *The Role of Fairness in Negotiation* by C. Albin.

by managing party interaction to ensure that the disputants respect each other's right to speak and opinions. For example, the mediator ensures that parties are not interrupted when expressing their concerns. The disputants will come to trust the mediator's advice if his or her comments and actions remain objective and relevant.

5.2.1.5 Listening actively

Mediators must be able to listen actively in order to understand the parties. In a conflict situation, communication is strained and the disputants tend to feel that they are not being either heard or understood. It is important that the mediator show the parties that he or she understands what they are saying, without siding with them. At the same time, the mediator must ensure that the other parties also understand the concerns being communicated. Active listening is a particularly effective communication tool.

This technique can be summarized as follows. After listening to the parties' concerns, the mediator summarizes the substance of their comments, expressing how they feel while eliminating any negative undertones. Suppose that during the course of a discussion a party suddenly bursts out: "Mr. X doesn't give a damn about us, he has no consideration for the citizens. He doesn't even have the decency to answer our letters!" The party being attacked will likely become defensive. When reformulating the first party's concerns, the mediator should reflect emotions in relation to the behaviour and not to the person so as to avoid assigning blame. The mediator could say: "Am I correct in saying that you're disappointed that your requests for information have gone unanswered?" Learning how to listen actively takes a lot of practice, and it is very useful for a mediator to develop this skill.

5.2.2 Helping parties work cooperatively

Interparty cooperation is rarely natural in a conflict situation. Many factors, including resentment and poor communication spoil relations. To create a positive dynamic for negotiation, the mediator must encourage the parties to work together or, at the very least, limit competition between them. Two strategies can be used to achieve this. The first focuses on communication and consists in fostering mutual understanding between the parties. The second entails dealing with negative attitudes. Figure 8 illustrates the mediator's actions in developing cooperation.

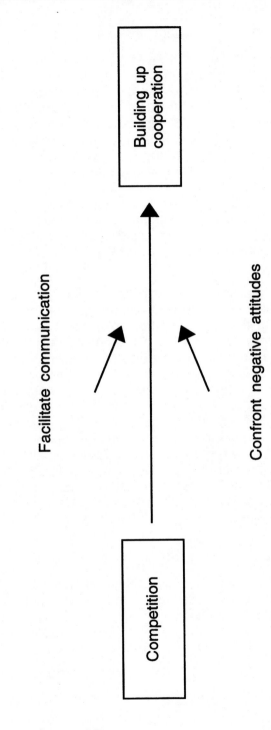

FIGURE 8

Development of cooperation

5.2.2.1 Facilitating communication

Communication between parties locked in conflict is usually characterized by distortions.[53] The mediator must regularly clarify and reformulate comments and proposals, since not all parties understand the proposal in the same way. Suppose, for example, that a promoter says a filtering station will limit the potential pollution of a river. The municipal representative may take that to mean that the promoter is going to pay for the station's construction, whereas the promoter is actually implying that the city should pay. By asking the promoter to specify who is to assume the costs of the station, the mediator can prevent a serious misunderstanding that could later lead to frustration and abort negotiations. It is important that the parties be asked to clarify any aspects of a proposal that may be ambiguous in order to ensure that everyone understands the same thing.

The mediator can also reformulate a proposal to make it more acceptable by eliminating blame and attacking the problem, thereby opening the door to other solutions. For example, a group of citizens may demand that a promoter install a filtering station to avoid polluting a river. The mediator could reformulate their demand as follows: "It is important to you that this project not pollute the river and, if I understand correctly, a filtering station would be an acceptable solution to the problem of industrial discharge. Is this correct?" This eliminates any blame, attacks the problem of pollution and leaves the door open for other solutions besides a filtering station. The mediator can even quiz the parties to see what they are willing to accept by asking them if they can think of any other options they might find acceptable. Any intervention directed at clarifying or eliminating aspects of a proposal to make it clearer and more acceptable can be considered a reformulation.

5.2.2.2 Dealing with negative attitudes

Parties with a negative attitude generally adopt an intractable negotiating position or intentionally hinder the mediation process. Resentment towards another party, which causes the above reactions, is normal and, to a certain degree, understandable in a conflict situation. Taken to the extreme, however, negative attitudes are

---

53 See *Defensive Communication* by J. Gibb.

incompatible with the cooperative effort needed to resolve a dispute and must be dealt with by the mediator.

Before deciding on the tactics to be used, the mediator must determine whether the parties are aware of these hostilities. In some cases, they are perfectly conscious of their negative attitude; in fact, their disruptive behaviour is part of their strategy.[54] In such instances, the mediator can confront the parties directly by asking them what they hope to accomplish. Do they really think they can influence the other parties by acting this way? Is there anything to be gained in the long run? The mediator should not hesitate to point out that highly negative attitudes are incompatible with mediation.

The situation is more delicate when parties are unaware of their hostility, which is manifested through more subtle behaviour that impedes the negotiation process. One such behaviour is that parties tend to look for problems that are not there. When this happens, the mediator must make them aware of their hostility by pointing out the inconsistency between their commitment to negotiate and their obstructive behaviour. The mediator can respectfully ask the parties to explain this contradiction in order to make them aware that their negative behaviour is hindering the process and then to deal with these attitudes as described above.

5.3   PRODUCTIVE PROBLEM-SOLVING

It is not sufficient to get the parties to the negotiating table; they also have to help formulate solutions. Unfortunately, the very fact that they are in conflict can dissuade active behaviour and prevent a consensual resolution. Active behaviour is linked to the parties' motivation to coordinate their efforts concretely and effectively. Whether or not they reach a consensus depends largely on the degree to which their interests are reconciled. The mediator can help the parties find a solution by assisting them in coordinating their efforts, favouring active behaviour, and reconciling their interests through a consensual solution.

---

54 Other obstructive, negative or misleading negotiation tactics are described in *The Negotiator's Handbook* by G. Fuller.

5.3.1 Active behaviour from the parties

What is active behaviour from the parties? First of all, when we say a person makes an active contribution to a project, it usually means that he or she participates in it. Participation is an important variable in active behaviour. Furthermore, it makes perfect sense that the degree of active behaviour is closely tied to the degree of party motivation. The more one feels that there is something to gain from mediation, the greater the incentive to invest in the process. Finally, in order for this active behaviour to lead to a settlement, the parties must commit to the negotiated solution. After all, a settlement is only useful if the parties agree to enforce it. Figure 9 illustrates the active behaviour triangle.

FIGURE 9

Active behaviour triangle

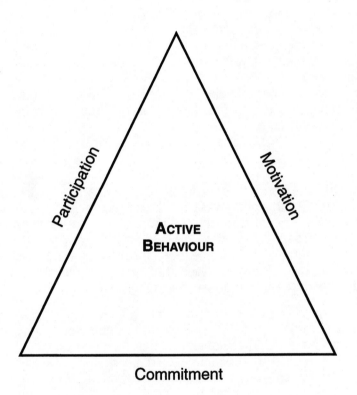

5.3.1.1   Participation

If a party feels neglected, it may refuse to support a consensus and thereby either unwittingly or voluntarily block a joint settlement in protest. While it is true that some parties may play only a minor role in the problem, an attempt should be made to involve them in the resolution process. The mediator can do this indirectly by consulting the parties on such things as procedure (scheduling of mediation sessions, joint sessions, caucuses, etc.). As a matter of course, the mediator can also ask the parties' advice on proposed options or solicit their feedback on how the negotiations are progressing. This way, even if a party does not participate in actually shaping a solution, it will feel like it is being consulted and contributing to the process. Consequently, it will be more inclined to support a consensus. Allowing the parties to take part in the dispute resolution process is the first step towards their active involvement in consensus-building.

5.3.1.2   Motivation

Classical research into social psychology has produced numerous studies on interparty cooperation. One of the most famous is Sherif and Sherif's.[55] One of the authors' most influential findings is that a common goal can be used to motivate two enemies to cooperate. In fact, according to them, the best incentive for cooperation is a "super goal". It is clearly obvious that this principle can be used to motivate the parties to resolve their differences.

There are two possible strategies for getting parties to work towards a common goal during mediated negotiation. First, the mediator can define an ultimate objective that exceeds and encompasses all other interests. An example would be ensuring a region's sustainable economic development. However, despite the noble attraction of an ultimate objective, it can be difficult to motivate parties to pursue something that, unfortunately, is for some often too abstract or idealistic.

The second strategy consists in identifying common elements in the parties' individual objectives and then building on them. Consider,

---

55 *Social Psychology* by M. Sherif and C.W. Sherif.

for example, a dispute over a project to construct a water system by raising the level of a lake. The contending parties may have very differing views and concerns about how to proceed, even though they share the common objective of supplying the community with drinking water. By focusing on this shared interest, the mediator can bring the parties closer together and encourage them to work cooperatively. It is no longer a matter of determining who is right, but of determining the best way to achieve a common goal while satisfying the parties' individual interests.

5.3.1.3   Commitment

Although a solution may look good on paper, making it official and implementing it may seem threatening to some parties. Getting them to commit to a negotiated settlement may be difficult. To begin with, any agreement in draft form may contain imponderables that hinge on future circumstances. Under these conditions, mutual trust between the parties is not always enough to secure commitment to the settlement. For example, some projects may be potentially harmful to the environment, in which case establishing responsibility for future impacts can be important. Promoter responsibility replaces trust as the basis for negotiation.[56] Thus, even if the impact assessment statement foresees no adverse effects, the promoter may nevertheless promise to install a filter in the smokestack should pollution levels become unacceptable.

Parties might also be reluctant to commit out of fear that a change in situation will put them at a disadvantage. Fear that the other party will force them to adhere to the agreement in an altogether different context acts as a deterrent. In this sense, it may be important for the mediator to suggest including a clause providing for renegotiation or remediation in the event of a substantial change in situation. These examples illustrate techniques for helping the parties commit to a settlement.

5.3.2   Consensus-building

Finding a solution is not an end in itself: the parties must also adhere to it. But obtaining unanimous support for a settlement can

---

56 On the trust-responsibility paradox, see *Sitting Controversial Facilities: Some Principles, Paradoxes and Heresies* by P.M. Sandman.

sometimes be harder than determining the best option. A party may hesitate to endorse a consensus for any number of reasons. It may be afraid of appearing weak and losing face if it retreats even a little from its opening position. It may fear that its members will find the agreement unacceptable. Or it may be afraid of setting a dangerous precedent that will compromise it during future negotiations. For these and many other reasons, it is important that the mediator employ tactics that encourage parties to support a consensus. Useful strategies include building on a change in situation, formulating an agreement that is acceptable to all parties and preserving party honour. Figure 10 illustrates the steps to facilitating settlement and consensus.

FIGURE 10

Facilitating consensus

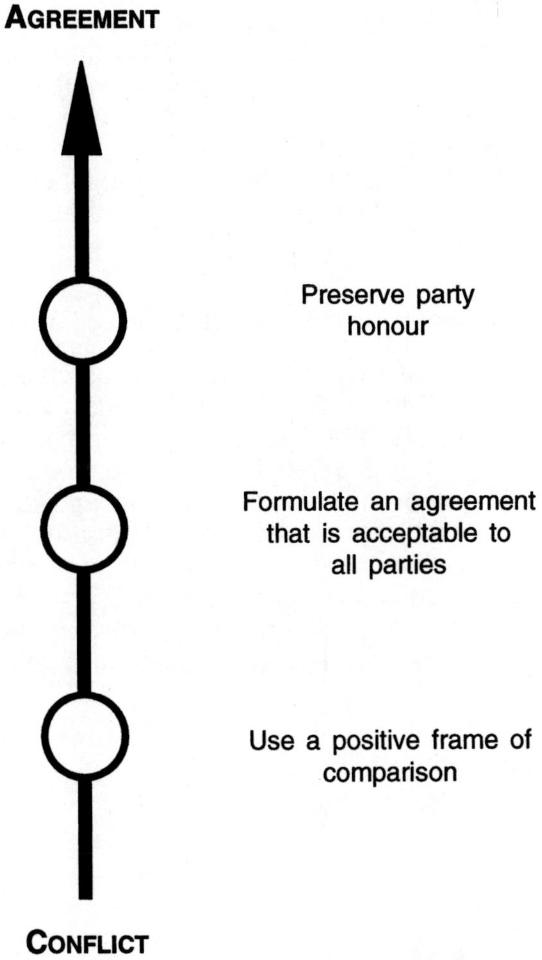

AGREEMENT

Preserve party
honour

Formulate an agreement
that is acceptable to
all parties

Use a positive frame of
comparison

CONFLICT

5.3.2.1 Using a positive frame of comparison

Successful negotiation necessarily results in change: the parties move from a conflict situation to a joint settlement. Party needs must be adjusted to fit this change. Unfortunately, disputants often tend to compare the negotiated solution with their ideal,[57] thus evaluating options in a negative light and downplaying their potential. If a party was initially seeking financial compensation of $25,000 and is offered $10,000, it might compare this offer against what it was expecting and see a loss of $15,000. This would be a negative evaluation.

One of the mediator's roles is to have the parties focus on what has been obtained in comparison to the initial situation. Continuing with the above example, the offer could be seen as a $10,000 gain in relation to what the party started out with, which was zero financial compensation. Using this approach, the mediator builds on the change in situation by assessing options in a positive light. The mediator stresses what has been gained in order to encourage parties to accept a settlement which is now perceived as an improvement over the initial situation.

5.3.2.2 Formulating an agreement that is acceptable to all parties

The way an agreement is formulated is of crucial importance, as it can either facilitate or discourage its acceptance by the disputing parties. Using an international or government standard as a criterion is one means of depersonalizing agreements. It is far easier for the parties to accept an objective criterion than an arbitrary one proposed by one of the disputants.[58] Neutral and objective decision-making promotes solutions that are acceptable to all parties, because the solutions are perceived as the logical outcome of the decision-making process and not as the result of pressure from one party. Helping parties formulate a neutral agreement is one of the mediator's primary tasks.

---

57 On framing proposals in the context of mediated negotiation, see *Negotiating Rationally* by M. Bazerman and B. Neale.

58 The use of objective standards is one of the four principles of principled negotiation. See *Getting to YES: Negotiating Agreement Without Giving In* by R. Fisher and W.L. Ury.

5.3.2.3 *Preserving party honour*

The importance of honour in accepting or rejecting a consensus should not be underestimated, be it simply to satisfy one's ego or for political gain. Although offhand these variables may seem tangential, they can constitute a major incentive for either adhering to an agreement or continuing the dispute. The mediator must ensure that any consensus preserves party honour.

The impact of this variable on the presentation of solutions can be illustrated using the analogy of a person selling pens. Suppose you buy a plastic pen from a peddlar for $4.00. If you tell your friends about your purchase, they may criticize you for having paid $4.00 for a pen worth no more than $1.00. However, if you tell them you agreed to pay that much because the profits go to charity, your friends may praise your generosity instead. Yet, in both cases, you paid the same price for the pen. It is all in how you present the situation. Similarly, in mediation, the mediator must remember that everyone likes to be seen as having a certain degree of leadership and a sense of pragmatism and fairness. Bearing these factors in mind when presenting agreements encourages parties to support the consensus.

5.4 HOW FINAL AGREEMENTS ARE REACHED

The ultimate goal of mediation is to resolve the dispute. In the previous chapter, we saw how mediation is used to assist parties in negotiating a settlement. In this chapter, we have explored how mediators can create a positive dynamic for negotiation. Now we will look at how final agreements are reached, or what constitutes a consensus. The way a consensus is reached obviously has considerable bearing on the dynamics of the negotiation process and depends on the mediation mandate. The mediator may be instructed to seek full consensus, i.e. the agreement of all parties, or partial consensus, i.e. the approval of a majority of parties. The type of consensus sought changes the dynamics of the negotiation considerably.

A full consensus requires the full cooperation of all parties. Everyone's needs become important and the end solution must satisfy the interests of all parties. In fact, consensus is only possible if all parties support the proposed solution, and this happens only when the solution benefits them. Although a full consensus generates far more integrative solutions than a partial consensus, it may be harder to negotiate. However, this should not deter municipalities or governments from using mediation to seek a consensual settlement in multiparty public disputes. In the state of Maryland, for instance, it took only 6 weeks for 110 citizens groups to reach a consensual agreement on recommendations for government management of solid waste.[59]

Sometimes an agreement that benefits the majority of players is prevented by the intractability, whether justified or not, of a single party. Suppose a city proposes to build a dam for its drinking water supply. If the city is already faced with a water shortage, the project could be vital as well as pressing. Now suppose different groups are fighting over the specifics of the project and a mediator has been called in to help resolve the dispute. During the negotiations, one of the parties adopts a hard-line stand and refuses to compromise, even though 90% of the participants have agreed to the changes made to the initial project. Should the project be allowed to go ahead even though there is only a partial consensus?

This is a difficult question to answer, especially since the situation is not always as clear-cut as the above example. It is easy to imagine that, although the goal should be an agreement that is supported by all parties, the situation may dictate otherwise. Mediating a partial consensus, on the other hand, can cause discussions to become divisive and lead parties to form coalitions, making negotiation even harder. Positions become extremely polarized, with coalitions generally adopting more hard-line stands than individual parties. It raises the question of whether the interests not compensated in the agreement are substantial enough to invalidate the agreement.

Not only can the type of consensus sought affect the dynamics of the negotiation process, it can also affect the relevance of the negotiated settlement. An agreement should balance maximum integration of all party interests with practical considerations. Before negotiations begin, the mediator and disputants need to agree on the criteria for a valid agreement, including what will constitute a consensual decision. The mediator should never underestimate the impact of the decision-making process on the dynamics of the negotiation process.

---

59 For details on this case, see *Maryland Reaches Accord on Solid Waste Issues* by B. Muldoon.

5.5   SUMMARY

Throughout this chapter, we have seen how the mediation setting sets the tone for the dynamics of the negotiation process. Two factors shape these dynamics. First, there are the interpersonal relations between the disputing parties, which are a function of mutual trust and cooperation. The mediator's role in this regard is to foster constructive dialogue. Second, the parties' active involvement and the search for a consensus contribute significantly to productive problem-solving. The role of the mediator here is to help the parties find a solution. The mediator intervenes at both levels to create a positive climate conducive to dispute resolution.

Although the process and dynamics of negotiation are two complementary aspects of mediation, they represent two very different types of intervention. The mediation process is linear, i.e. a step-by-step procedure with the same steps being followed for all mediation unless the mediator and disputants decide otherwise. In contrast, the dynamics of the negotiation process are case-specific and the mediator's actions must be adapted accordingly.

The mediator's interventions will vary with each case. He or she must be able to read and adjust to different situations. Knowledge and understanding of the mode of intervention proposed in this chapter can help the mediator diagnose the dynamics of the negotiation and help him or her decide on appropriate action. Finally, the context of mediation in public disputes also affects the process and dynamics of negotiation, as we will see in the next chapter.

Chapte

Ethics and Tra

CHAPTER 6

ETHICS AND TRANSPARENCY

6.1 A SPECIAL FRAMEWORK

In the foregoing chapters, we explored the various elements involved in a mediation effort designed to reconcile interests in public disputes. We defined mediation, the role of the mediator and the procedure, and examined the dynamics of the negotiation process. We now need to define the framework for applying mediation to public disputes so that the process can be adapted to suit the specific context of public conflict management.[60] The judicial process and public hearings, for example, are governed by a code of procedure as well as a code of ethics. If mediation is supposed to be the extension of traditional dispute resolution techniques, then it is only logical that it, too, be governed by a moral code.

Furthermore, given the considerable impact public disputes and their settlement have on the communities concerned, management must be based on the principle of transparency, meaning that the information needed to understand the issues must be made public. Citizens have a right to be informed of decisions that affect their quality of life. In this regard, mediation again draws from traditional dispute resolution methods which over the years have developed mechanisms for ensuring that the information process is transparent. However, since mediation is a relatively new approach to conflict management, it would be simplistic to think one can take established codes of ethics and transparency mechanisms and apply them to mediation. This chapter seeks to establish the foundations of a code of ethics and a transparent information process which, while based on other management methods, are specific to the mediation of public disputes.

---

60 For an overview of the distinct features of public dispute mediation, see *Comparaison entre la médiation administrative et publique appliquée dans le domaine de l'environnement et la médiation privée* by P. Renaud.

6.2　CODE OF ETHICS

Can you imagine what would happen if mediators acted on a whim or allowed themselves to be swayed by economic, political or partisan influences? The disputants would be uncertain of what to expect, would hesitate to openly discuss their needs, and would fail to participate actively in negotiations. They would be distrustful, and with reason. For mediation to be successful, it is vital that the mediator be neutral and respect certain rules in order to gain the trust of the parties and communities affected by the decisions that are made.

A code of ethics is a valuable, essential tool for framing the mediation process. Its primary purpose is to provide mediators with guidelines for overall intervention; in a sense, it tells mediators what to do and what not to do. However, it would be pretentious to propose a definitive code of conduct in this chapter, since rules vary depending on the dispute and the organization offering mediation services. The following are guidelines for the content and organization of a code of ethics which is appropriate for public mediation, yet open-ended.[61]

6.2.1　Elements of a code of ethics

What should be included in a code of ethics for public mediation? The best way to answer this question is to identify the concerns such a code must address. The first is efficiency. Is mediation an efficient way to manage the conflict? The second is the mediator-party relationship. Is the mediator impartial and have the parties made an enlightened commitment to resolve their differences? Third, the interests of individuals affected by the dispute but who are not taking part in the negotiations must be respected; in particular, the interests of the general public. Figure 11 illustrates the constituent elements of these three ethical considerations.

---

61 For a general description of the elements of a code of ethics, see *Thoughts on the Development of a Code of Ethics in Mediation* by P. Renaud.

FIGURE 11

Pyramid of ethical principles
of public mediation

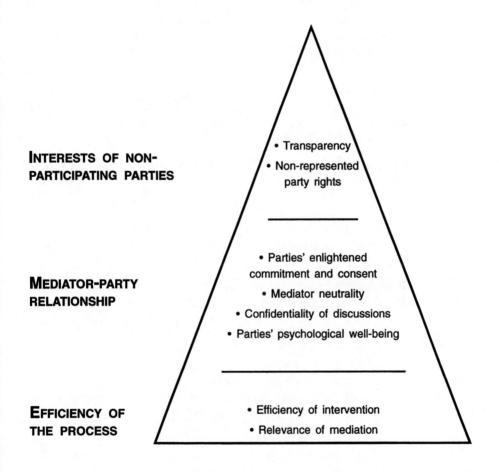

6.2.2 Efficiency of the process

Mediation is not always the best course of action and should not be chosen lightly. The mediator must determine whether it is a good conflict-management choice. Is the dispute suitable for mediation and can it be resolved through face-to-face negotiation? Mediation may not be the best way to handle the conflict, which is where relevance comes in. If the mediator feels resolution is possible, he or she must have the ability and experience to see the process through. If the mediator does not feel capable of managing the conflict efficiently and effectively, he or she should refer the case to another qualified mediator, or work with that person. If the case is not suited for mediation, the mediator must advise the parties of other means of resolution. Efficiency and relevance are the two primary elements of ethical mediation.

6.2.3 Mediator-party relationship

The decision to engage in mediation must be an informed one. The parties should fully understand the different stages in the process, the mediator's role and the negotiation procedure. As well, the mediator must make sure the parties grasp the significance of their commitment to a settlement agreement before signing it. In short, the principle of party autonomy must be coupled with the principle of informed decision-making.

The mediator-party relationship must be impartial. In other words, the mediator must remain neutral when allowing the parties to speak, making procedural decisions, commenting on proposed solutions, and acting otherwise during negotiations. The mediator also needs to be discreet, and respect the confidentiality of the process. The mediator may be privy to certain information or become the disputants' confidant. The information conveyed must remain confidential, unless the parties specifically ask the mediator to serve as go-between. However, confidentiality must be balanced with transparency (see Section 6.3).

Furthermore, the mediator is somewhat responsible for the tone of the negotiation and the disputants' psychological well-being. He or she must set clear ground rules: insults, blame and threats must not be tolerated. The mediator must also ensure that the parties respect each other's viewpoints and that the parties pace is not unduly forced. In other words, mediation should not be a traumatic experience for the parties.

6.2.4   Interests of non-participating parties

Some individuals and groups that may be affected by the dispute and the decisions rendered might not be at the negotiating table. The classic example of this is future generations. Even if a new plant creates thousands of jobs in the short term, what kind of social, cultural or environmental heritage will it leave for generations to come? A more immediate example is citizens who were not initially concerned by the project or policy, but who would be affected if modifications were made during negotiation. This is what is meant by respecting the rights of non-participating parties. No matter how good the disputants' intentions are, the mediator must act as their social conscience when it comes to respecting the rights and interests of affected parties who are not involved in the discussions.

In the same vein, all relevant information pertaining to negotiated solutions must be transmitted to the public. Agreements reached during the course of mediation can affect entire regions, and the population has a right to be informed. Restricting information that concerns communities or regions to a privileged group would be unethical in the case of public conflict. Consequently, in addition to ensuring that third-party rights are respected, the mediator must make sure the process is sufficiently transparent. This aspect is discussed below.

6.3   ORGANIZATION OF A CODE OF ETHICS

The elements of the code of ethics proposed in this chapter are presented in hierarchical form (Figure 11). This type of structure is useful for informing mediators about the appropriate course of action in a given situation. For example, if the parties agree to a project that will have significant adverse effects on the community, should the mediator conform to the principle of confidentiality or to that of non-represented party rights? According to the pyramid of ethical principles, non-represented party rights are more important and the mediator should inform the parties that he or she cannot morally "ratify" the agreement and may even have to publicly disapprove of it should the parties decide to proceed against his or her advice.

At first glance, this type of intervention may seem drastic, even inappropriate, in relation to party autonomy. However, the public nature of the conflict must be taken into consideration. The goal of mediation in a public dispute is not to favour one party over another, but to help the parties find a creative solution while respecting the interests of citizens. Lawrence Susskind has delved at length into the social responsibility of mediators.[62] In his opinion, given the interests at stake, the mediator has a responsibility to protect future generations. Therefore, according to the pyramid, respecting citizens' interests takes precedence over the mediator-party relationship.

In the same vein, the mediator-party relationship takes precedence over efficiency (Figure 11). It would not be ethical for the mediator to disregard the principle of confidentiality on the pretext that divulging information would make the process more efficient. A hierarchical organization ranks the three principles underlying a code of ethics, i.e. efficiency, the mediator-party relationship, and protection of the interests of non-participating parties. It must be remembered that a code of ethics is a guideline designed to complement, not replace, sound judgment.

6.4   TRANSPARENCY

There must be a certain degree of transparency in the management of public disputes. As previously mentioned, such disputes impact significantly on the population, and citizens have a right to be informed. The same rule applies to mediation: the process must be sufficiently transparent to inform the public on the issues at stake and the reasons for decisions.

The fundamental question is, what information should be disclosed and what information should remain confidential? Where do you draw the line between the private and the public character of mediation? In principle, all information needed to understand decisions made during the mediation of a public dispute should be public, while emotions, such as anger or frustration, and any other information that could compromise a party, should remain confidential. Although the

---

62 See *Environmental Mediation and the Accountability Problem* by L. Susskind.

process should be transparent, public mediation ought not to become a source of public entertainment.

To help understand the notion of transparency, the types of information disclosed during mediation can be divided into categories. First, there is information pertaining to procedure, such as the dates of mediation sessions, phases and steps involved in the process, objectives for negotiation, etc., in other words, the transparency of the process. Then there is the content of mediation sessions, or the transparency of discussions. Finally, settlement decisions and the substance of agreements, which can be public information, are subsumed under transparency of decisions.

While the issue of what is public and what is private is by no means black and white, at the very least, it is reasonable to want the decision-making process to be transparent. A certain degree of transparency in the mediation process enables interested citizens to follow the progress of negotiations and to become familiar with the mediation procedure. On the other hand, the necessary transparency of discussions is very much a grey zone, and it is up to the mediator, the disputants and the organization overseeing the mediation to decide on an appropriate procedure. Since releasing the content of discussions can suppress spontaneity, it is important that the mediator balance transparency with efficiency.

6.4.1   Disseminating information

While it is relatively easy to demonstrate the relevance of transparency for public dispute mediation, determining the means for disseminating information is not. Several variables must be considered when choosing a communications strategy. What information should be disseminated, i.e. procedural decisions and/or the content of discussions and/or decisions? How widely should the information be distributed: a community, a region, a province or even a state? A number of other more practical but nevertheless important variables must also be taken into account. The communications strategy necessarily has an impact on the mediation process. Table 8 compares various means for disseminating information to the public.

TABLE 8

Comparison of information dissemination methods

MEANS OF DISSEMINATION / CHARACTERISTICS	PRESS RELEASES	MINUTES OF MEETINGS	TRANSCRIPT OF SESSIONS	PRESENCE OF PUBLIC	PRESENCE OF MEDIA	TELEVISED SESSIONS
Transparency of process	+/-	+/-	+	+	+	+
Transparency of discussions	-	+/-	+	+	+/-	+
Transparency of decisions	+	+	+	+	+	+
Distribution of information	Average	Limited	Limited	Average	Wide diffusion	Wide diffusion
Impact on process	Minimum	Minimum	Average	Significant	Significant	Significant

6.4.2   Press releases

Clearly, press releases are the simplest and probably least expensive way of disseminating information. As negotiations progress, the mediator releases information on the procedure or on decisions taken by the parties. A group composed of representatives from each party can be formed to act as spokespersons. In addition to being both easy and inexpensive, press releases maintain maximum confidentiality while distributing key information to the public, thereby ensuring efficiency. However, since the information published is generally only a summary of what took place, it can undermine transparency. Also, the range of distribution may be restricted, as publication of the press releases will depend on media interest.

6.4.3   Minutes of meetings

Another means of disseminating information is to publish the minutes of negotiation meetings. Essentially, minutes are an enhanced form of press release. In addition to reporting decisions, they help increase the transparency of the process and the operational procedure adopted by the mediator and parties, and ensure a modicum of transparency in discussions. Since only the substance, and not every word, of discussions is reported, the mediator and parties can filter information, thereby ensuring the disputants of a certain degree of confidentiality and reducing potential impacts on the mediation process. As with press releases, a multiparty group can be formed to draft the minutes. Given that minutes are simply placed somewhere where they are available for public consultation, the distribution is limited.

6.4.4   Transcript of mediation sessions

Transcripts of mediation sessions are another way of ensuring transparency. Discussions are stenotyped and the transcripts made available to the public. They generally provide information on the process, the content of discussions, and decisions. Since every word is recorded, there is greater transparency. Furthermore, transcripts constitute written proof of what occurred during sessions, which can be useful later on. On the other hand, the same instruments used to increase transparency can cause parties to hold back for fear that they may be compromised. The experience of Québec's environmental hearings office (BAPE), which uses this method, has nevertheless shown that disputants are able to engage in frank discussion despite the stenotypist's presence. As with minutes, distribution is more limited than with press releases, since transcripts must be consulted on site.

6.4.5   Presence of the public

Since most trials are open to the public, mediation could conceivably be open to the public as well, with interested citizens attending sessions. While this would make the entire process completely transparent, the lack of confidentiality could make the parties extremely tense, thereby discouraging spontaneity and creativity. It is not surprising that certain cases mediated using this approach have ended in a stalemate.[63] Working out their differences before an audience tends to inhibit the parties' faculties and can greatly reduce, if not preclude, efficiency.

6.4.6   Presence of media

Another way to communicate information to the public is to allow journalists to witness the mediation process. Through their respective media, they can inform the population of developments, exchanges and decisions. Reach is thus far wider than with any of the methods previously described. Although the presence of the media can make the disputing parties extremely reluctant and apprehensive to participate in negotiations, the experience has been positive in a number of cases, particularly in the United States.[64] Journalists were able to rally the population, change attitudes toward the dispute, and promote a better understanding of the negotiated settlements. How successful this approach is, however, obviously depends largely on the journalists, and whether they are looking to stir up controversy or to help the population understand the problem. Although media presence is not very popular to date, it can prove worthwhile provided it does not impede efficiency.

---

63 The impact of public and media presence on the mediation process is discussed in *The Media: Friend or Foe? Working Out Media-Mediator Relationships* by K.L. Khor.
64 *Ibid.*

6.4.7   Televised sessions

Televised sessions are an extension of public and media presence. From limited distribution to the public present in the room, information becomes accessible to the entire population of a given geographical area. On the other hand, the disadvantages of public presence increase tenfold with televised sessions, not to mention the high costs involved. While the total transparency and the vast dissemination of information this approach allows make it the ultimate means of transmitting information to the public, the disastrous experience and media frenzy generated by certain high-profile cases may be cause for reflection on the relevance of bringing television cameras into mediation sessions.

6.5   CHOOSING A COMMUNICATIONS STRATEGY

Choosing a communications strategy is a crucial step in the mediation of public disputes. Although it is vital to gaining public confidence in the process and in decisions, it can also create tension between the disputants. One party may prefer or even demand that the public be present, while another may want press releases only. It is up to the mediator to define the proper balance between the degree of confidentiality required for negotiations to be productive and the degree of transparency required to keep the public adequately informed.

The strategies discussed in this chapter are not mutually exclusive. They are complementary and can be combined to devise a specific communications plan tailored to each case. Although determining the best strategy may be difficult, the choice should be guided by an evaluation of what is relevant to the public's understanding of the case, while ensuring the process is efficient.

For example, during the first three phases of the mediation process, news releases could be published and the minutes made available to the public. The final agreement could be announced at a press conference in order to inform the population of decisions and get its reactions. If necessary, a poll could even be conducted to determine to what extent the public approves the settlement. The possibilities are endless, and the mediator and disputing parties must be innovative in formulating the communications plan. Finally, when determining the right strategy, it is important to remember that par-

119

ticipants in the mediation process come to the table with emotional baggage. In this sense, the process should never be allowed to become a public spectacle; if it is, negotiations will fail and the primary objective of mediation, i.e. the reconciliation of interests, will be unattainable.

6.6   SUMMARY

In this chapter, we have explored the notion of a code of ethics for mediation in public disputes. The advantage of such a code is that it establishes a standard of conduct for mediators and, by extension, for mediation procedure. The special context of public disputes requires that the mediator's activities conform to certain standards. The code of ethics proposed here is based notably on three fundamental principles: efficiency, the mediator-party relationship and respect for the interests of non-participating parties. Where this last principle is concerned, the notion of transparency is particularly important. Unlike private disputes, which are settled in total confidentiality, public disputes require a certain degree of transparency, since the negotiated settlement affects more than just the negotiators.

There are several ways to inform the public of the negotiations and ensure the process is transparent. The differences between the strategies identified in this chapter lie mainly in how much and how widely information is distributed, and whether or not observers are present during mediation sessions. There is no one way to proceed; it is up to the mediator to develop a strategy that suits the dispute.

The different ethical considerations and the need to disseminate information highlight the complexity of mediation in public disputes. Mediators working for an organization such as a private or government mediation office have the resources needed to respect these considerations. Of course, this organization must have its own strict code of ethics as well as a public information policy based on transparency. This does not mean, and it would be unwise to assume, that an independent mediator cannot properly mediate a public dispute. On the contrary, an ad hoc body or committee can be struck for the specific needs of the case at hand. In fact, an ad hoc body or committee can be far more suitable and flexible than a permanent organizational structure. The important thing to remember is that public dispute mediation is really a multidisciplinary task and that the mediator should work with a team in order to create a setting conducive to conflict resolution that reflects the public interest.

Conclusion

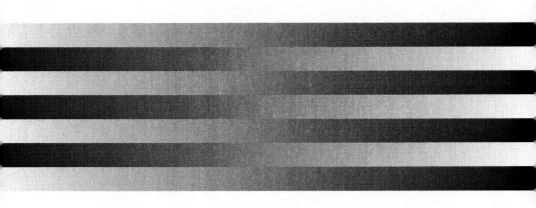

CONCLUSION

With endless government spending cuts and a virtual moratorium on new projects, today's political motto is "do more with less." While this is easier said than done, it does reflect reality. Future generations will probably have to make do with fewer resources, since it is unlikely, at least in the short term, that government budgets will be restored to their former glory. Whether we can do more with those resources will depend on how we choose to resolve the conflicts that arise from this new situation. Very likely, tremendous tension between interest groups whose achievements or future developments are threatened will arise.

Mediation is one of the most promising dispute resolution method. It minimizes the cost of conflict, while maximizing the social benefits of cooperation, making it possible to do more with less. For this reason, it is important that public administrators, interest group leaders, universities and the public at large become familiar with the process of mediation in public disputes. This does not mean that we should all become mediators, but rather that there should be no qualms about requesting mediation or engaging in the process.

Mediation definitely has a promising future. In his popular book *Megatrends: Ten New Directions Transforming Our Lives*, John Naisbitt identified two trends that appear to be crystallizing as the 20th century draws to a close. First, we are seeing a major societal shift from a representative democracy to a participatory democracy, in which citizens are participating more and more in decisions regarding projects or public policies. Second, single solutions are giving way to a new paradigm of multiple solutions: the future lies not in "either/or", but in "and". It is no longer a matter of having to choose between solution 1 and solution 2, but of reconciling the underlying interests in order to craft a solution that is acceptable to all involved. Mediation not only echoes these two trends, it fosters their full expression.

As a management tool, mediation is more than just a new approach to public dispute resolution. It is also a vehicle for social change,[65] as it reinforces the social function of conflict, promotes the involvement of communities in resource management, and develops a certain social capacity for innovative dispute resolution. Furthermore, our North American democratic tradition is rooted in public town meeting,[66] where citizens meet to discuss neighborhood issues and agree on how to solve problems. In this regard, mediation and the reconciliation of interests in public disputes is a way of getting back to basics.

---

65 See *Public Conflict Resolution: A Transformative Approach* by F. Dukes.
66 See *Politics for People: Finding a Responsible Public Voice* by D. Mathews.

Bibliography

BIBLIOGRAPHY

ALBIN, C., "The Role of Fairness in Negotiation" (1993) 9:3 *Negotiation Journal* 223.

BARUCH BUSH, R., "Efficiency and Protection or Empowerment and Recognition: The Mediator's Role and Ethical Standards in Mediation" (1989) 41 Florida L. Rev. 253.

BAZERMAN, M., and B. NEALE. *Negotiating rationally*. New York: Free Press, 1992.

BLACKBURN, J.W. "Environmental Mediation As an Alternative to Litigation: The Emerging Practice and Limitations." In *Alternative Dispute Resolution in the Public Sector*, edited by M.K. Mills. Chicago: Nelson-Hall Publishers, 1991.

BOSKEY, J.B., "The Proper Role of the Mediator: Rational Assessment, Not Pressure" (1994) 10:4 *Negotiation Journal* 367.

BRESLIN, J.W., and J.Z. RUBIN. *Negotiation Theory and Practice*. Cambridge: PON Books, 1991.

Bureau d'audiences publiques sur l'environnement. *Autoroute 55 : doublement de la chaussée entre Bromptonville et l'intersection avec le chemin de la Rivière*, Rapport d'enquête et de médiation n° 71. Québec: BAPE, 1993.

Bureau d'audiences publiques sur l'environnement. *Construction du poste de distribution Roussillon à 315 kV-25 kV et d'une ligne de dérivation biterne à 315 kV à Laprairie*, Rapport d'enquête et de médiation n° 78. Québec: BAPE, 1994.

Bureau d'audiences publiques sur l'environnement. *Programme décennal de dragage aux abords des quais de Cargill Limitée à Baie-Comeau*, Rapport d'enquête et de médiation n° 70. Québec: BAPE, 1993.

Bureau d'audiences publiques sur l'environnement. *Projet d'assainissement des eaux Pointe Fisher Ouest, Ville de Lac Brome*, Rapport d'enquête et de médiation. Québec: BAPE, 1992.

Canadian Environmental Assessment Agency. *Sandspit Small Craft Harbour Mediation Process*. Ottawa: CEAA, 1995.

CHAUVEL, A.M. *Résoudre un problème : méthode et outils pour une meilleure qualité*. Paris: Dunod, 1992.

COBB, S., "Empowerment and Mediation: A Narrative Perspective" (1993) 9:3 *Negotiation Journal* 245.

COSER, L. *The Function of Social Conflict*. New York: Free Press, 1956.

DE BONO, E. *Six chapeaux pour penser*. Paris: InterEditions, 1987.

DEUTSCH, M. *The Resolution of Conflict: Constructive and Destructive Processes*. New Haven: Yale University Press, 1973.

DUKES, F., "Public Conflict Resolution: A Transformative Approach" (1993) 9:1 *Negotiation Journal* 45.

FIELD, P., "Quality Dispute Resolution: How Can You Be Assured of Quality Service?" (1994) 22 *Consensus* 4.

FISHER, R. "Playing the Wrong Game?" In *Dynamics of Third Party Intervention: Kissinger in the Middle East*, edited by J.Z. Rubin, 95-122. New York: Preger, 1981.

FISHER, R., and S. BROWN. *Getting Together: Building Relationships As We Negotiate*. New York: Penguin Book, 1989.

FISHER, R., and W.L. URY. *Getting to YES: Negotiating Agreement Without Giving In*. Boston: Houghton-Miffin, 1981.

FOLBERG, J., and A. TAYLOR. *Mediation: A Comprehensive Guide to Resolving Conflicts Without Litigation*. San Francisco: Jossey-Bass, 1984.

FULLER, G. *The Negotiator's Handbook*. Englewood Cliffs (New Jersey): Prentice Hall, 1991.

GIBB, J. "Climate for Trust Formation." In *T-Group Theory and Laboratory Method*, edited by L. Bradford, J. Gibb, and K. Benne, 279-309. New York: Wiley, 1964.

GIBB, J., "Defensive Communication" (1961) 11 *Journal of Communication* 141.

HONEYMAN, C., "Five Elements of Mediation" (1988) 4:2 *Negotiation Journal* 149.

HONEYMAN, C., "On Evaluating Mediators" (1990) 6:1 *Negotiation Journal* 23.

JOHNSON, R.A. *Negotiation Basics: Concepts, Skills and Exercises*. Newbury Park (California): Sage, 1993.

KHOR, K.L., "The Media: Friend or Foe? Working Out Media-Mediator Relationships" (1994) 24 *Consensus* 4.

KOLB, D.M. *The Mediators*. Cambridge: MIT Press, 1983.

KUNREUTHER, H., "Moving Communities from 'NIMBY' to 'YIMBY'" (1992) 15 *Consensus* 1.

LAX, D.A., and J.K. SEBENIUS. "Interests: The Measure of Negotiation." In *Negotiation Theory and Practice*, edited by J.W. BRESLIN, and J.Z. RUBIN, 161-180. Cambridge: PON Books, 1991.

MADIGAN, D. *et al. New Approaches to Resolving Local Public Disputes.* Washington: National Institute for Dispute Resolution, 1990.

MATHEWS, D. *Politics for People: Finding a Responsible Public Voice.* Urbana: University of Illinois Press, 1994.

MATZ, D.E., "Mediator Pressure and Party Autonomy: Are They Consistent with Each Other?" (1994)10:4 *Negotiation Journal* 359.

MOORE, C.W. *The Mediation Process: Practical Strategies for Resolving Conflict.* San Francisco: Jossey-Bass, 1986.

MULDOON, B., "Maryland Reaches Accord on Solid Waste Issues" (1993) 18 *Consensus* 1.

NAISBITT, J. *Megatrends: Ten New Directions Transforming Our Lives.* New York: Warner Books, 1982.

POITRAS, J. *La médiation : le rôle et la dynamique de la confiance entre les parties.* LL.M. Thesis, Laval University, 1993.

PRUITT, D., and J. RUBIN. *Social Conflict: Escalation, Stalemate and Settlement.* New York: Random House, 1986.

RAIFFA, H., "Post-Settlement Settlements" (1985) 1:1 *Negotiation Journal* 9.

RENAUD, P., "Comparaison entre la médiation administrative et publique appliquée dans le domaine de l'environnement et la médiation privée" (1994-95) 25:1-2 R.D.U.S. 345.

RENAUD, P., "The Environmental Assessment Process and Public Participation in Québec: Concrete Elements for Sustainable Development" (1996) 27:3 R.G.D. 375-393.

RENAUD, P., "Environmental Officials in Quebec Serve as Mediators" (1994) 24 *Consensus* 8.

RENAUD, P. "La médiation en environnement au BAPE : un processus administratif et public." In *Développements récents en médiation (1995).* Cowansville: Éditions Yvon Blais Inc., 1995, 117.

RENAUD, P., "La médiation et les conflits entourant les projets d'infrastructures routières" (1996) 743 *Revue générale des routes et des aérodromes S.A.* 20-25.

RENAUD, P., "Thoughts on the Development of a Code of Ethics in Mediation" (1995) 5 *ADR Forum: The Canadian Journal of Dispute Resolution* 2-5.

RUBIN, J.Z., "Some Wise and Mistaken Assumptions About Conflict and Negotiation" (1989) 45:2 *Journal of Social Issues* 195.

SADLER, B., and P. JACOBS. "Définir les rapports entre l'évaluation environnementale et le développement durable : la clé de l'avenir." In *Développement durable et évaluation environnementale : perspectives de planification d'un avenir commun.* Ottawa: Canadian Environmental Assessment Research Council, 1990.

SANDMAN, P.M., "Sitting Controversial Facilities: Some Principles, Paradoxes and Heresies" (1992) 15 *Consensus* 2.

SAUNDERS, H.H., "We Need a Larger Theory of Negotiation: The Importance of Pre-Negotiating Phases" (1985) 1:3 *Negotiation Journal* 249.

SHERIF, M., and C.W. SHERIF. *Social Psychology.* New York: Harper and Row, 1969.

SMITH, W.P., "Effectiveness of the Biased Mediator" (1985) 1:4 *Negotiation Journal* 363.

Society of Professionals in Dispute Resolution. *Competencies for Mediators of Complex Public Disputes.* Washington: Society of Professionals in Dispute Resolution, 1992.

SUSSKIND, L., "Environmental Mediation and the Accountability Problem" (1981) 6:1 Vermont L. Rev. 1.

SUSSKIND, L., and J. CRUIKSHANK. *Breaking the Impasse: Consensual Approaches to Resolving Public Disputes.* New York: Basic Books, 1987.

TOUVAL, S., "Multilateral Negotiation: An Analytic Approach" (1989) 5:2 *Negotiation Journal* 159.

URY, W.L. *Getting Past No: Negotiating Your Way from Confrontation to Cooperation.* New York: Bantam Books, 1993.

URY, W.L., J.M. BRETT, and S.B. GOLDBERG. *Getting Disputes Resolved: Designing Systems to Cut the Costs of Conflict.* Cambridge: PON Books, 1993.

WEST, N., "Estuarine Quality Use and Public Perception" (1987) *Coastal Zone '87* 804.

WORCHEL, S., J. COOPER, and G.R. GOETHALS. *Understanding Social Psychology.* Pacific Grove (California): Brooks/Cole Publishing Company, 1991.

ZARTMAN, I.W., "Common Elements in the Analysis of the Negotiation Process"(1988) 4:1 *Negotiation Journal* 31.

ZILLESSEN, H., "So You Want to Be an Environmental Mediator? Survey Shows Preparation Must Include Classroom and 'School of Hard Knocks' " (1996) 29 *Consensus* 5, 8.

INDEX